FROM NEGATIVE TO POSITIVE

(In My Own Words)

By Davon McNeil

Freebird Publishers
Box 541, North Dighton, MA 02764
Info@FreebirdPublishers.com
www.FreebirdPublishers.com

From Negative to Positive (In My Own Words)
By Davon McNeil

Publisher & Distributor: Freebird Publishers
Box 541 North Dighton, MA 02764
Web: FreebirdPublishers.com
E-Mail: diane@freebirdpublishers.com
Corrlinks: diane@freebirdpublishers.com
JPay: diane@freebirdpublishers.com
Toll-Free: 888-712-1987
Phone/Text: 774-406-8682
Send Letters to the Editor to the above address

All Freebird Publishers titles, imprints and distributed lines are available at special quantity discounts for bulk purchases for sales promotions, premiums, fundraising educational or institutional use.

ISBN: 1548897973

ISBN-13: 978-1548897970

Printed in the United States of America

I Will Never Allow This Negative History To Define Me.

CRIMINAL HISTORY

The following criminal history was obtained from McNeil's Massachusetts Board of Probation:

Juvenile

Court	Offense	Arraignment Date	Disposition
Plymouth Juvenile	Distribute/Dispense Class B (crack cocaine)	April 22, 1994	DEL-DYS-SS
Roxbury Juvenile	Knowing Rec Stolen Prop	September 1, 1992	DYS-SS
Plymouth Juvenile	Assault and Battery	June 12, 1992	Prob-DYS-SS
Plymouth Juvenile	Knowing Rec Stolen Prop	June 9, 1992	Prob-DYS-SS

Adult

Court	Offense	Arraignment Date	Disposition
Plymouth Superior Court	Murder 2nd Degree	October 24, 2000	Committed Life w/Parole
Fall River District	Poss Class A/ Heroin	October 25, 1999	Guilty 90 days CMTd
Fall River District	Poss Class B/ Cocaine	October 25, 1999	Guilty 90 days CMTd
Brockton District	Poss Class D	February 24, 1999	CWOF & Court Cost
Brockton District	Shoplifting	February 24, 1999	CWOF & Court Cost
Brockton District	Knowing Rec Stolen Prop/ MV	March 14, 1996	Guilty-2 years-SPS- 90 days-probation terminate
Brockton District	A & B Dangerous Weapon (Gun)	December 21, 1995	Dismissed
Brockton District	Assault to Kill	December 21, 1995	Dismissed
Brockton District	Firearm Violation Carry w/o License	December 21, 1995	Dismissed
Brockton District	Firearm Violation w/o Poss FID Card	December 21, 1995	Dismissed
Brockton District	Firearm Violation W/I 500 feet Dwelling	December 21, 1995	Dismissed
Brockton District	Trespassing	September 19, 1995	Guilty File
Brockton District to Brockton Jury	A & B Dangerous Weapon	July 7, 1995	Guilty 2 years CMTD
Brockton District	Distribute/Dispense Class D	June 5, 1995	DF/Guilty 1 days CMTD
Brockton District	Conspiracy to Violate Cont Sub Act	June 5, 1995	DF/Guilty File
Brockton District	Control Substance School Zone	June 5, 1995	DF/Guilty 2 years CMTD
Brockton District	Poss to Distribute Class D	June 5, 1995	DF/Guilty 1 days CMTD
Brockton District	Poss to Distribute Class B	May 3, 1995	DF/Guilty 1 days CMTD
Brockton District	Conspiracy to Violate	May 3, 1995	DF/Guilty 1 days CMTD

	Cont Sub Act		
Brockton District	Control Substance School	May 3, 1995	Guilty 2 years CMTD
Brockton District	Carrying Dangerous Weapon	September 15, 1994	Guilty 1 years CMTD
Brockton District	Poss of Firearm/ No Fid	September 15, 1994	DF/Dismissed
Brockton District	Carrying Dangerous Weapon		DF/Guilty 1 years CMTD
Brockton District	Poss of Firearm/ No Fid	September 15, 1994	DF/Guilty 1 years CMTD
Brockton District	Larceny of MV	September 12, 1994	Dismissed
Brockton District	Knowingly Rec Stolen Prop	September 12, 1994	CWOF-DFW-Guilty 2 years SPS 1 year CMTD & Term

Who would've ever thought?

PREFACE

"A legitimate redemptive effort to change yourself takes arduous discipline to succeed. So making a positive transition in your life is a sign of strength, never weakness." – *Tookie Williams*

In The Name of Growth and Development

I have maintained a state of positive, institutional adjustment throughout my incarceration. I have dedicated my time in prison to the work of establishing rehabilitation. I have sought out, completed and participated in many activities, groups and programs that focus on, and target, the correction of criminal-addictive thinking and behaviors.

I have directly targeted the most significant risk areas that influenced the criminality which led to my incarceration.

In the beginning of my incarceration I asked myself, "How did I get here?" During the therapeutic process and responsibility of answering that question, I came to the understanding of "how to stay out of prison." It was through a determined path of rehabilitation that has manifested in me a healthy process of transformation, stability and a life that is lawful. This will insure the success of my reintegration back into society, parole conditions and obedience of the laws of the land. I've grown into a state of mature masculinity. I have also held steady employment throughout my entire incarceration. I've been studious in the concept of work as therapy, education, conditioning and training myself for the routine and maintenance of the responsibility of civil living.

I have also been accepted into the "Inmate Worker" program at BSH (Bridgewater State Hospital). It is a privilege given to individuals who meet the criteria of continuous, positive, institutional adjustment and lack of disciplinary issues. Every tool and skill that I have learned has become a part of my thinking and behavior today. These are skills which I practice in my day-to-day life, and will continue to practice once I am released.

FROM NEGATIVE TO POSITIVE

Table of Contents

Part I: Author Biography

Part II: Transcending the (6)! (My Transition from negative to positive)

Part III: New Program Proposals by Davon McNeil

Part IV: The Journey

DEDICATIONS

Nation of Gods & Earths, Eye internalized the divine teachings of our father (Allah) and sealed them within my heart. Through actuating said teachings Eye was victorious in the task of liberating myself from the mental darkness. The (20) is the light & the light is the TRUTH!

Allah Fu-Quan, Eye can never thank U-God enough for blessing 1-7 with the keys (Supreme Mathematics & Supreme Alphabets) which Eye utilized to open the door (120°). U-God made (1) (9) that Eye was the greatest and the kingdom of God was to be manifested through my Arm Leg Leg Arm Head. Also, it was U-God who told me Eye was the sole controller of my destiny, the author of my reality. We waste no time searching for that which does not exist.
Eye love U-God, Peace!

Melanie, I love you supremely. When I was lost within those streets, you were my reason for finding my way home at night. My masculinity is divinely balanced by your femininity (smile). Yes, we've experienced many trials and tribulations, but through it all our true love remains strong. Thank you for being supportive of me during my many crucibles. And I always tell you: you're the best mother in the world.

Juel, you will never fully understand the hell I've gone through to arrive at this stage in my life. I only want the best for you. You call it preaching; I call it teaching (smile). Please cherish the jewels (wise words) that I'm constantly blessing you with. Regardless to whom or what, never allow life to dictate your direction. You're the creator of your destiny. I love you. Baby.

Shalese, life is a precious gift; but we're solely responsible for the unwrapping of it. You've carved out a journey for yourself and you're living it out to the best of your ability. I want you to always look within and seek out the greatness at the core of your being. Never, never, never allow anything or anyone to prevent you from achieving your goals. I love you. Little Lady.

To all of my little brothers, sisters and cousins, I'm sorry for not being the big brother/cousin that I was supposed to be. I allowed the streets to swallow me up. But this book is a testament to my growth and development and victory over my past life. You all gave me the strength and motivation to continue moving forward. I love you all.

To all of the volunteers who came through the many iron gates and steel bars to help us men find direction while guiding us towards rehabilitation, I sincerely thank you. You provided us with a number of great programs; teaching us how to find our true selves. When many in society said no, you said yes. You were able to see past our crimes; you saw us as human beings. I'm forever grateful. This book is dedicated to you. Thank you so much.

To all of my supporters who continue to stand tall by my side, I truly thank you and appreciate you. You're a tremendous source of strength and energy for me as I traverse this mountain. Mr. Haywood Fennell, Sr., I want to thank you for your wise council (smile).

PART ONE

Author Biography

1

CHAPTER ONE

AUTHOR BIOGRAPHY

My full name is Davon DaShawn McNeil. I was born on July 29, 1977 in the city of Boston, Massachusetts at Boston Children's Hospital. My mother gave birth to me at the age of sixteen. I was born prematurely by two months. Being born prematurely caused me to experience a few complications: bladder and kidney infections and a heart murmur. The doctor told my mother he could tell I was a fighter and had a strong will to survive. My complications forced me to remain hospitalized in an incubator for approximately two months.

My father was seventeen years old at the time of my birth. He had recently been released from a juvenile detention facility and would visit me in the hospital with a group of his closest friends. They would cause trouble by riding in wheelchairs up and down the hospital hallways; smoked marijuana inside the hospital bathrooms; and would stuff five, ten and twenty dollar bills through the openings of my incubator. When the nurses would come to check on me and clean me up, I would be covered in piles of money.

Before I turned two years old my father was incarcerated. From that point forward, prison would become the norm for my father, leaving my mom to raise two young boys on her own. My mother worked two jobs so that she could provide for me and my little brother. Therefore, we spent the majority of our young lives at our grandparent's home. They were very loving, caring and extremely hardworking individuals. They owned a house and a building which were located next to each other. One was a single family dwelling and the other one could accommodate three families. In addition to my father, my grandparents have two daughters:

Meta and Debora Archie.

My two aunts played a huge role in my upbringing and were a strong influence on my pliable young mind. When my aunts were in their mid to late twenties they wanted their independence. So my grandparents rented them the third floor apartment in the building they owned next door. I was nine, maybe ten years old when my aunts moved into their apartment. This period began the process of shaping, molding and conditioning my young mind to learn a way of life which would ultimately lead me down a path of utter destruction; causing my family, community, innocent members of society and myself a great amount of heartache and pain.

My aunts were well-known to all the people of the underworld (the streets). Their third floor apartment became the local hangout for individuals who were defying the law and living the fast life. On the weekends the apartment would bustle with heavy foot traffic as a result of the poker, blackjack and dice games which would be taking place. It was common for me to see large sums of money being counted, drugs being cooked and used, and guns lying around in various places. My father's closest friends would be there and would always give me crispy five, ten and twenty dollar bills. I would frequently retrieve cold beers for all the gamblers, earning those crispy bills.

It was during these gatherings I would hear stories about my incarcerated father. I would sit quietly and listen intently as my father's friends would regale me with stories of his criminal lifestyle. They would tell me how I looked just like him; how he was a sharp dresser and a serious lady's man. As I listened I would fantasize about becoming exactly like my father. My aunts would explain to me—in vivid detail—how they would stuff my diaper with an assortment of drugs and smuggle them into various prison facilities where my father sold the drugs for money and food to survive. These stories were told in an excited and positive manner.

Therefore, these stories became firmly rooted within my young mind. I was determined to make my father proud of me by becoming just like him.

In 1989, at the age of twelve years old, my little brother, mother and I were living with my maternal grandmother when she passed away. Her passing forced my mother to scramble to find us a place to live. We ended up in Brockton, Massachusetts, living with my maternal grandfather. I clearly remember my mother sitting me down and explaining our sudden move to a new city; assuring me everything would be all right. She told me Boston was getting progressively worse with all the gang violence and Brockton was a safer place for us to reside in. My mother was also concerned about the negative effect my father's friends were having on me. She didn't realize that everything I was being exposed to by my aunts and my father's friends were already embedded within my young mind.

Our first apartment in Brockton was on Glenwood Street which at the time was a very quiet and laid-back neighborhood. But right around the comer was Spring Street which was infested with drugs and violence. So I entered the sixth grade at Arnmone Elementary School. I met a young man named Thomas (Boodah) Coward (now deceased). We became fast friends because we shared a similar upbringing. Boodah's older brother, Rack, was a well-known drug dealer and their older sister, Leah, had a boyfriend who also dealt drugs. Boodah's mother and father would hold poker tournaments at their Highland Street home. I was allowed to spend the weekends there and the atmosphere was extremely familiar. I had been raised in the same type of environment.

I formed a strong bond with Boodah's older brother and began to hang out more with him. He introduced me to a lot of his friends who were all drug dealers; all had criminal records and carried guns. Some of them had served time in prison. Being around Rack and his friends reminded me of my father and his friends. I loved being in their presence. They always had on brand new clothing and sneakers; drove nice vehicles; had pockets full of money; and all the girls were attracted to them. I wanted to be just like them.

Due to my mother's work schedule, I had a lot of free time to spend with my friends.

Most of my childhood friends were being raised by single mothers due to their father's being incarcerated or just absent. My father was serving a ten-year prison sentence. While most kids were riding their bikes or playing video games, I was on Spring Street selling crack cocaine and carrying guns. That negative culture (way of life) would become my everyday reality until July 24, 2000 when I was arrested and charged with first-degree murder.

THE CRIME

On July 17, 2000, I left my mother's apartment on 20 Grand Street in a Brockton taxi cab headed to 30 Fuller Street to sell crack cocaine. Upon arrival, I encountered between ten to fifteen individuals. I walked into the driveway directly across from 30 Fuller Street where I stashed my drugs and a .38 caliber gun I was carrying that day. When I walked back across the street an associate of mine, Fred Philippe, asked if I wanted to take a ride with him and smoke some weed. His car was parked in the driveway of 30 Fuller Street and we entered the vehicle; he drove and I was in the passenger seat.

Another associate of ours, Tremalle Clark, rode his bicycle over to the driver's side of the car. He stuck out his hand and clutched the driver's side mirror as we began to drive off. He told Fred to speed up; all three of us laughing as the car increased speed for about twenty feet. Fred told Tremalle to let go of the mirror but he refused. But he eventually let go and rode around to the front of the car. We were not driving that fast so Tremalle was pedaling slowly. However, he began to speed up and then he would suddenly pedal slowly again and then speed up again. He kept doing this and as a result, Fred would have to quickly press down on the brakes whenever Tremalle dropped his speed. At one point, Fred couldn't stop the car in time and hit the back tire of the bike, causing Tremalle to fall off. Visibly upset, he jumped onto the hood of the car and proceeded to jump onto the windshield which caused it to shatter. Glass flew all over Fred and I which instantly incited our anger. Fred got out the car and started arguing with Tremalle. I got out and pushed myself between them to prevent a physical altercation.

I turned toward Tremalle, shouting, "Look what you've done!" while pointing my finger at the shattered windshield.

He yelled back, "Mind your own fucking business." And as we continued to exchange heated words, Fred got back into the car and drove off. Tremalle ran in the opposite direction and I walked back to 30 Fuller Street.

Fred returned about fifteen minutes later, dressed in all black and riding a bicycle. He asked me where was Tremalle and I told him he had run off. Thinking Tremalle might return I retrieved my gun from across the street. But as soon as I returned to the driveway, a red car pulled up to the stop sign at the comer of Fuller and Bartlett Street and Tremalle jumped out of the passenger side and immediately started shooting at Fred and I. We pulled out our guns and began to shoot back. Tremalle jumped back into the car and it sped away. Fred and I ran away from the scene as well.

Two days later, around noon on July 19th, Fred picked me up at my mother's apartment. He explained that Tremalle, Bruce Montrond and Dennis Jordan were riding around, looking for us. So we drove to Fred's house where I left my gun two days prior. We sat in his driveway, smoking marijuana, before Fred went into his apartment to retrieve my gun. With no specific destination in mind, and without saying a word to each other, we headed in the direction of Fuller Street. As we pulled into the driveway of 30 Fuller Street, five to eight persons were standing around smoking marijuana. Fred got out of the car and walked over to the group. I stayed in the car. After about ten minutes had passed, a dark green car pulled up and Dennis and Bruce got out of the car. I did the same when I saw them.

Dennis and Bruce squared off with Fred and me. Bruce's aggression was obvious when he spoke, "What the fuck happened the other day between you and my man Mal (short for Tremalle)?"

I responded with similar aggression and told him, "What happened has nothing to do with you so stay out of it!"

He said, "It has everything to do with me because Mal's like my little brother and if I had a gun on me we wouldn't be having this conversation right now!"

Hearing that, Dennis reached into his waistband and took a few steps backwards. Then Fred yelled, "He got a gun!"

Out of fear, anger and stupidity I pulled out my gun and shot recklessly at Bruce, hitting him twice. Fred and I ran to the car and sped away. I stashed the gun in a wooded area along Pine Grove Drive and we headed to Fred's girlfriend's apartment. I left Fred there and drove to my grandmother's house in Boston. My grandmother must have sensed something was wrong because as soon as she opened the door she immediately asked me if everything was all right. I broke down and started to cry. She hugged me and asked what was wrong. I told her I had just shot someone. I looked my grandmother in the eyes and explained to her everything which had happened. She told me I should turn myself in and leave it in God's hands.

I laid down on her couch in the living room and eventually fell asleep. When I woke up I had thirty missed calls from Fred on my cell phone. I called him back and he told me Bruce had died. I hung up and sat there thinking about the past three days of my life. Later, Fred called again to say he had to come get the car because it was a rental and he had to return it. I gave him directions to my grandmother's house and an hour later he was there to pick up the car. He told me the police were all over the city and I should be careful. Then he gave me some money and left.

I stayed with my grandmother for the next five days. And on the fifth day, July 24, 2000, the police showed up, looking for me and I was promptly arrested and charged with first-degree murder. I awaited trial in the Plymouth House of Corrections. It took three years and four months before I was brought to trial and convicted of second-degree murder on September 15, 2003.

This Will Not Be My Legacy!

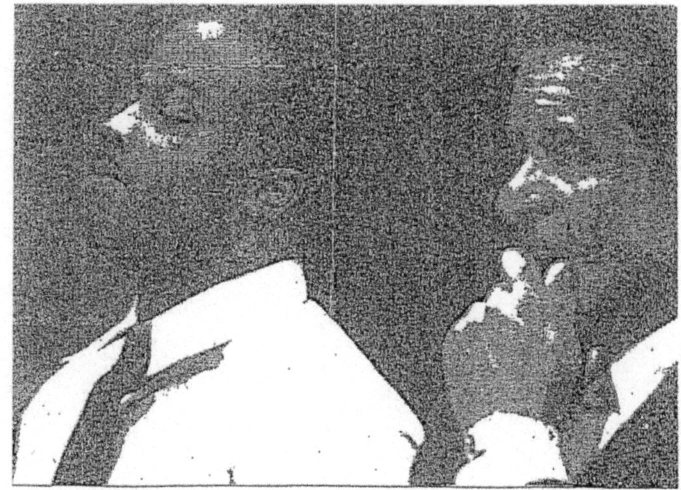

CRAIG MURRAY/THE ENTERPRISE

DEFENDANT DAVON D. McNEIL listens as he is found guilty of the murder of Bruce Montrond in Brockton Superior Court Monday. McNeil was sentenced to a life term in prison. Defense attorney J. Drew Segadelli is at right.

Jury convicts McNeil

After deliberating 5½ hours, a jury finds a Brockton man guilty of Bruce Montrond's murder.

By Maureen Boyle
ENTERPRISE STAFF WRITER

BROCKTON — As his mother choked back sobs, Davon D. McNeil was convicted in the shooting death of a 20-year-old Brockton man three years ago.

After deliberating 5½ hours, the jury convicted McNeil, 26, of second-degree murder Monday afternoon in the slaying of Bruce Montrond as the defendant's relatives and friends packed the second-floor courtroom at Brockton Superior Court.

Judge Richard J. Chin sentenced McNeil to the mandatory life in prison with a chance of parole after serving 15 years. McNeil will receive credit for the three years in jail awaiting trial, meaning he will be eligible for parole in 12 years.

Extra police officers were called in to keep watch

GUILTY/Page A4

A4 The Enterpr

Jury finds man guilty

GUILTY/From Page A1

both inside and outside the Belmont Street courthouse, just blocks from where the fatal shooting occurred July 19, 2000, amid fears of a confrontation between the defendant's family and friends and relatives of the victim after the verdict.

As the jury filed in, McNeil lowered his head and stood quietly as the guilty verdict was read.

Assistant District Attorney Patrick O. Bomberg told the judge Montrond's mother, knowing McNeil would receive a mandatory sentence, declined to provide a victim impact statement as allowed by law.

"She does not feel she needs to address the court," he said.

McNeil, formerly of Grand Street, was arrested less than a week after Montrond was shot to death in broad daylight on Fuller Street in Brockton.

Montrond was fatally wounded after what prosecutors said was an argument with McNeil. One of the people who was with Montrond the day he was shot was Dennis F. Jordan, a Brockton man now jailed on a string of violence charges.

Friends drove Montrond to Brockton Hospital after the shooting. He later died at the hospital.

Two people identified McNeil as the gunman during the trial.

Four members of Montrond's family were in the courtroom as the verdict was read. His mother, Estela, wiped away tears.

A contingent of McNeil's family and friends sobbed after the verdict was read, and his distraught mother was helped by relatives from the courtroom.

The verdict came about three hours after jurors asked the judge to define "reasonable doubt" when weighing the charges.

Defense attorney J. Dr[ew] Segadelli said the jury appeared [to] have weighed the evidence ca[re]fully by failing to find his clie[nt] guilty of the more serious charge [of] first-degree murder.

"There seemed to be sor[ne] doubt they had," he said. "Unfort[u]nately, not enough."

Maureen Boyle can be reached mboyle@enterprisenews.com

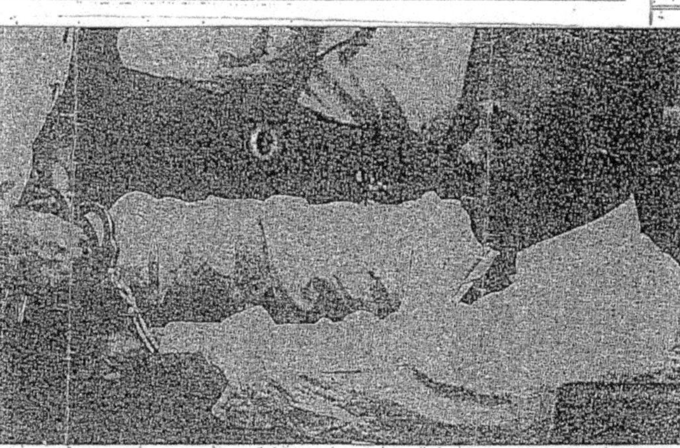

CRAIG MURRAY/THE ENTERPRI[SE]

DEFENDANT DAVON D. McNEIL has handcuffs removed before the verdict in for the Bruce Mo[n]trond murder trial. McNeil was found guilty in Brockton Superior Court Monday. McNeil was se[n]tenced to a life term in prison.

3

CHAPTER THREE

CURRENT VIEW OF THE CRIME

I have come to the complete realization that, sixteen years ago, I committed the worst crime in existence — I selfishly stole a young man's life and took him away from his family and friends. I had no right to shoot and kill Bruce Montrond. I had a social responsibility to tell someone about the deep-rooted anger settled at the center of my being. I held my anger inside of me where it burned quietly. I fully and completely understand I had been shut up within my own mental darkness, thus becoming an unconscious accomplice in my own subjugation; becoming my own worst enemy. I lived each day with reckless abandon, not fearing or caring about tomorrow. I had a false sense of invincibility and for many years I participated in my own dehumanization.

After ten years of constant and deep reflection, I've been able to heal the wounded inner- child. I never imagined that within me, at my core, was a scared, angry and hurt child. My consistent, negative and reckless lifestyle made me numb and afraid to acknowledge my internal world. Ten years ago I made a conscious choice, a legitimate redemptive effort to change my entire life for the better. I refused to allow that ominous and destructive lifestyle to hold me within its foul, wretched and deadly embrace.

A strategy began to take shape within my mind: I was going to become the voice of positive affirmations every day for myself, other prisoners, correctional officers and staff. My conscience began to shine its light within an environment firmly rooted in negativity and eternal darkness. Today, my entire life is dedicated to being of service to my inner-self and others. Being able to transition into a pro-social lifestyle has allowed me to heal from the ignorance of my past. I've undergone a personal transformation by being able to connect with the deepest part of my personality; the part that thinks and reasons and doesn't get triggered into aggression or defensiveness. Every day I do the work of re-examining my childhood suffering to deal with the past so I can move on with greater self-respect, freedom and creative power. Telling the truth about myself and my past has brought my heart and true self back to life. I will spend the rest of my life telling the truth about my past.

4

CHAPTER FOUR

EVERYDAY RULES AND LAWS BY WHICH I LIVE MY LIFE

1. I can make choices in my life everyday which will nurture the tree of non-violence and wither the tree of violence.
2. Reach for that something in others which seeks to do good for self and others.
3. Help "build" community based on honesty, respect and caring.
4. Expect the best from yourself.
5. Don't rely on weapons, drugs and alcohol; they weaken you.
6. Make friends with persons who will support you. Support the best in them.
7. The world we have created is a product of our thinking. It cannot be changed without changing our thinking.
8. Seek to resolve conflicts by reaching common ground.
9. When you are clear about your position, expect to experience great inward power to act on it. A response which relies on this power will be courageous and without hostility.
10. Build your own self-respect.
11. Ask yourself for a non-violent way. There is one inside of you.
12. Risk changing yourself.

5

CHAPTER FIVE

MY APOLOGY

First, I would like to extend my sincerest and deepest apology to the entire Montrond family. I especially want to apologize to Bruce Montrond's mother and father for the tremendous amount of grief, suffering, pain and devastation that I, Davon McNeil, caused you on that tragic day of July 19, 2000 at 12:30 p.m. when I selfishly shot and killed your son, Bruce Montrond. On that day I was a coward; a savage; a young punk who hid behind a .38 caliber revolver. I had absolutely no right to take Bruce's life away from you and your family. I am truly sorry for what I have done. I want you to know I take full responsibility for my actions. I need for you to know and understand that Bruce had nothing to do with my deep-rooted anger and intense self-hatred that manifested itself on that fateful afternoon. Bruce didn't do anything wrong. Bruce was a victim of my severe irresponsible and undisciplined lifestyle. Bruce and I exchanged heated words, and those small words were enough to cause me to lose control and pull out my gun and shoot Bruce twice. Again, please know that Bruce didn't do anything wrong. It was me — Davon McNeil. I am the young man who is solely responsible for killing your son, Bruce. I was wrong. It was and is my entire fault. I now understand the fullness of my actions.

I can never give back the gift of Bruce's life that I so recklessly stole away from you. There is nothing I can say or do to relieve you of the pain and hurt and destruction I've brought to you and your family. I can only beg for your forgiveness. Please forgive me for what I've done. Please forgive me for being selfish. Please forgive me for taking Bruce's life. I am truly sorry. Please forgive me.

6

CHAPTER SIX

TO MY FAMILY

I want to apologize to my entire family. I was not born a murderer, a drug dealer, a criminal nor was I raised to commit thoughtless harm. I was raised within a family structure where deep love, morality, values, discipline and work ethic were in place and expected to be lived out by each member of the family from the oldest to the youngest. However, there was a shadow element within our family which was founded on ignorance, lies, neglect, misguidance, falsehoods and deceit. It was this shadow element I matriculated through at a very young age; at an age where I wasn't cognizant of right or wrong. I was socially engineered into believing that selling drugs, smoking marijuana, carry guns, utilizing foul language, stealing, lying, defying the law and going to jail, prison and funerals were normal activities and were supposed to take place.

I don't blame nor do I point my finger at any family member for the revelation made above. Today, I understand I was "misinformed by the misinformed." You were passing on to me what was passed on to you by your elders. But what was passed on wasn't right! There is a vicious cycle which exists within our family that needs to be completely destroyed. We have to rid ourselves of the negative emotions which continue to be stumbling blocks to our path of forgiveness. Whether we want to consciously acknowledge it or not, the denial and repressed expression of sorrow, like any repressed emotion, will present itself in another form. The sorrow can be masked as chronic emotional and physical symptoms: depression, anger, hostility, unhealthy shame, guilt, addictions, etc. Or it can show itself as apathy, disguised by an "I don't care" attitude. Am I lying or am I telling the truth?

Having revealed all of the above, I can still say there is a love that permeates within our family which has existed as our foundation for eternity. As you read these words of wisdom, close your eyes and reflect upon the historical gathering of our souls. We're the forever people, without beginning or end. I apologize with divine love. I love you, family.

PART TWO

Transcending the (6)!

(My Transition from Negative to Positive)

7

CHAPTER SIX

REHABILITATION

Rehabilitation: What is rehabilitation? The concept of rehabilitation rests on the assumption that criminal behavior is caused by some factors. This perspective does not deny that people make choices to break the law, but it does assert that these choices are not a matter of pure "free will." Instead, the decision to commit a crime is held to be determined, or at least heavily influenced, by a person's social surroundings, psychological development, or biological makeup. People are not all the same and thus free to express their will, but rather are different. These "individual differences" shape how people behave, including whether they are likely to break the law. When people are characterized by various "criminogenic risk factors"—such as a lack of parental love and supervision, exposure to delinquent peers, the internalization of antisocial values, or an impulsive temperament—they are more likely to become involved in crime than people not having these experiences and traits.

The rehabilitation model "makes sense" only if criminal behavior is caused and not merely a free-willed, rational choice. If crimes were a matter of free choices, then there would be nothing within particular individuals to be "fixed" or changed. But if involvement in crimes is caused by various factors, then logically re-offending can be reduced if correctional interventions are able to alter these factors and how they have influenced offenders. For example, if associations with delinquent peers cause youths to internalize crime-causing beliefs (e.g. "it is okay to steal"), then diverting youths to other peer groups and changing these beliefs can inhibit their return to criminal behavior.

The following documents will show and prove my rehabilitation. It is being presented as evidence of the person I am today and will, without a doubt, reveal how I've spent my time in prison and the transformations I've made in my life. I did not waste time in any way, shape or form. I left no stone unturned. I did not try to "run away from myself." I confronted myself mentally, emotionally and spiritually. I established and nurtured healthy and strong relationships. I learned and trusted the concept of work as therapy and education. I "lived" in programs, learned a trade (public speaking) and educated myself. I also, after learning the psychology of how to rehabilitate myself, helped others to do the same. By learning to resist my lower-self, which manifested learned destructive habits, I was able to construct a realm of positive desires.

After my physical release from prison, I will have to contend with being a man—a black man—with a State murder conviction on my record, which is the worst conviction; other than convicting myself. This will place me in the second-class citizen zone. The truth is, this is a reality I have proactively prepared for and today I am ready and able to successfully navigate my way in society.

I have overcome my greatest obstacle: myself. I am no longer in my former state of mind, character or culture which can no longer entice me to commit crime on any level.

I have become an agent of lasting change; helping our youth to not fall victim to negative culture (the streets) and the criminal-addictive thinking which has me sitting in prison today. I am ready to live the rest of my life as a responsible and productive citizen of the world.

My best work of art is my own life which I will forge and live out according to my own creative will. My will gives me the power to create as well as gives me the ability to aspire beyond what is immediately available. Will is the power of choice!

Positive Education Always Correct Errors! Peace.

IN THE GENESIS

In the genesis of my journey through prison, I was blessed to meet a few sages (wise men) who granted me free transportation into their schools of divine wisdom. These men were considered scholars amongst the prison population and were held in high regard by the prison administrators. They were deemed model prisoners who navigated the labyrinth of prison life with a quiet disposition and erect posture. Through rain, hail, sleet, or snow you could always find these men in the prison yard, training intensely, mastering their physical bodies through the use of calisthenics and jogging. But it was in the small confines of dingy, unventilated and cluttered 8'xlO' cells where the talents of these men shone brightly. Scattered about those dungeon-like cells were books, paper, pens, pencils and a number of huge dictionaries and thesauruses. Each of these men owned a personal library of sacred tomes and encouraged me to develop my reading muscle and develop an unquenchable thirst for knowledge. In those cells is where I was taught the discipline of mind-over matter and how to rise above the atmosphere of stagnation, misery, violence and mediocrity which permeated the prison environment. I enjoyed steaming cups of green tea mixed with a pinch of ginger and a dollop of honey while being instructed in the art and science of "fasting." Fasting was highly recommended to serve as a means to purify the body and promote the development of an extraordinary degree of self-discipline, control and willingness to sacrifice for the achievement of goals. Each of these men taught me valuable lessons; and I would utilize these lessons many years later to achieve my freedom from prison. Let me share a few of them (not all) with you: 1) Listening - paying attention with my brain, eyes and ears (third eye); 2) Concentration - being able to focus intently with my "minds-eye" on what is being said, done, or studied without distraction; 3) Remembering - developing the ability to recall and/or recite all important details of discussions, speeches, lessons and pictures; and 4) Memorizing - developing the ability to retain, organize and present in order all facts, information and knowledge when questioned. I sincerely thank those wise men who allowed me to enter their schools of divine wisdom. Forever sealed within my heart is the knowledge, wisdom and understanding they shared with me. Peace is the way of the righteous!

"When the student is ready, the teacher will appear."

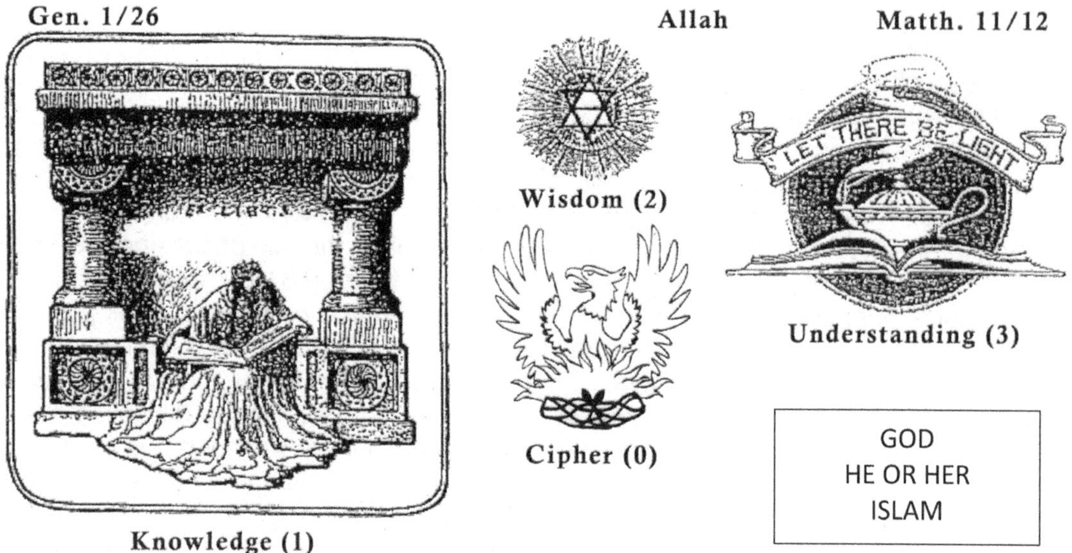

The world has always been divided between two leading groups; the truth seekers and the truth supressors. The truth seekers endeavor to free the masses from the darkness of ignorance and give them light (truth). The truth suppressors seek to enslave the masses by destroying light (truth) and keeping them in darkness.

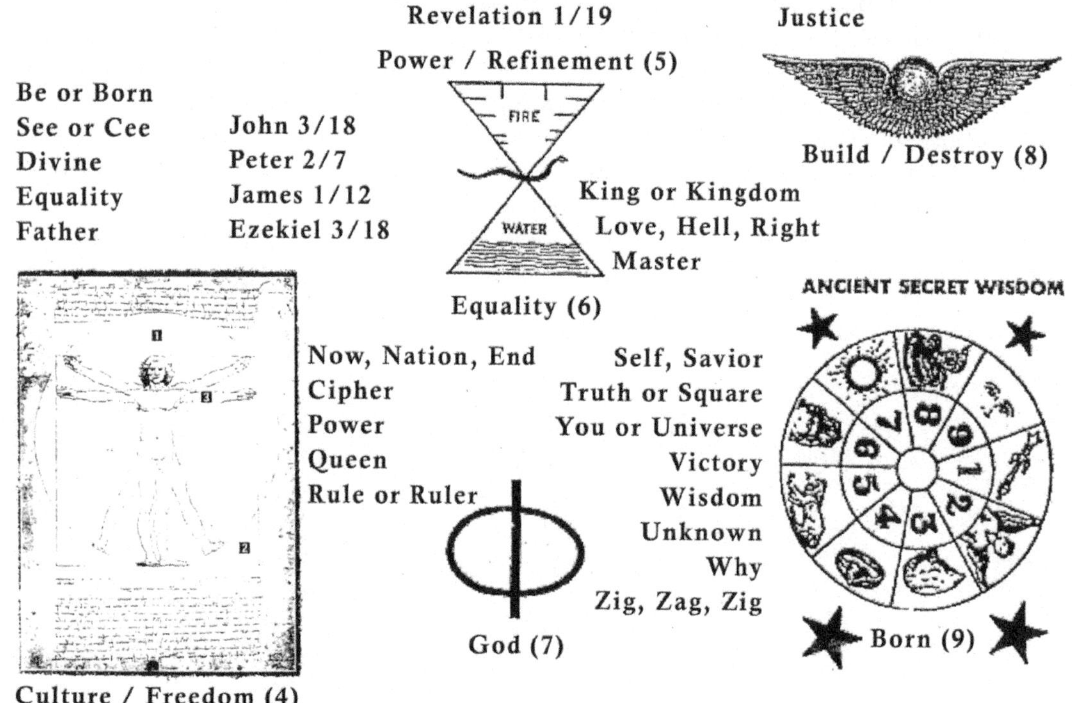

Smart Recovery Program

SMART RECOVERY

Self Management and Recovery Training

CERTIFICATE OF COMPLETION

Davon McNeil W-82395

December 1, 2010

This certificate is awarded for the participation
and successful completion of the Smart Recovery Program

Christine Brockelman, Director of Treatment

The Smart Recovery Program is a no-nonsense men's work program that assist men in institutional and community settings who have broken the law. We're taught to face difficult truths about ourselves so that we can identify and pursue more productive directions in our lives.

My experiences in Smart Recovery has reinforced in me the reality that, "I am so much more than the worst act that I've committed." The graphic and extreme contents of this program have helped me to have a greater respect for life and the care of people. It made me grateful for having and learning from my experiences in life so I could better appreciate that I now have the opportunity to live as a productive citizen once my debt to society is paid. I will live my life as a reformed and righteous man.

Correctional Recovery Academy (CRA)
Graduate Support Program (GSP)

Certificate of Completion

A collaborative program of the Massachusetts Department of Correction & Spectrum Health Systems, Inc

This certificate is awarded to

Davon McNeil

for successfully completing the ***Correctional Recovery Academy***

on this 16th *day of* December 2010

Because we know that our lives matter, that we can be greater than our circumstances, that we can return good for harm, we therefore humble ourselves to learning. Our graduation is a true commencement - let us begin anew.

Director of Treatment

CRA Supervisor

The Correctional Recovery Academy (CRA) and Graduate Support Program (GSP) are the best programs I've experienced in my sixteen years of incarceration. The CRA operates as a six month, twenty-four hours a day, seven days a week, structured and therapeutic community which targets criminal-addictive thinking and behaviors. It provided me with the tools I needed to maintain my sobriety.

I successfully graduated from the program in December, 2010. This program assisted me in my determined idea to retire from my criminal-addictive thinking and negative behaviors. In January 2013, I was accepted into the Graduate Support Program. I was given the responsibility of being a mentor and a facilitator of the CRA curriculum to men battling criminology and addiction on many levels. It helped me to make a cultural adjustment in my life.

I was able to manifest my new outlook (positive) on life and not just talk about it. You cannot fake your change, especially around career criminals and addicts. I facilitated several classes: motivating behavioral change, core skills, steps for intervention, recovery concepts and components. Many of these topics helped me in establishing change in my life on a deep and personal level. I also discovered my passion to build constructive communication with other men and CRA staff members. I helped many men in their personal fight and mission to recovery.

Alternatives to Violence

Certificate

Workshops for Training in Nonviolence

Alternatives to Violence Project / New England

Awards this Certificate to

Davon McNeil

Who has satisfactorily completed the Basic Course in

Nonviolent Conflict Resolution

January 7, 2011

Facilitators Date

The Alternatives to Violence Program (AVP) has helped me in methods of transforming power and conflict resolution. I've also benefited greatly by my work as a facilitator and advocate of the AVP over the course of my incarceration. Today, when I am triggered by something, I immediately investigate my thoughts. I've grown to learn that there's a lesson to be learnt in the emotions that rise to the surface, whether positive or negative.

I learned to fight against the inner feelings of anger and violence. I practice healthy, constructive thinking in order to manifest my desires. This education and training will indeed benefit me tremendously in my life after incarceration. I make choices in my life every day that will nurture the tree of non-violence and wither the tree of violence. I've also learned to work towards new ways of overcoming injustice. I'm willing to suffer suspicion, hostility, rejection and even persecution, if necessary, to rid myself of all negativity.

Smart Recovery Program
(Renewal)

My Second Completion...

SMART RECOVERY

Self Management and Recovery Training

CERTIFICATE OF COMPLETION

Davon McNeil W-82395

March 23, 2011

This certificate is awarded for the participation and successful completion of the Smart Recovery Program

Christine Brockelman, Director of Treatment

I decided to attend the Smart Recovery Program a second time to renew and refresh myself with the teachings and lessons within the program. I've come to the divine realization that opening up to people and sharing my past life has allowed me to create a bond with other men whom I normally wouldn't associate with. Sharing with others has also granted me an opportunity to heal old wounds.

Alternatives to Violence Program (Advanced)

Certificate

Workshops for Training in Nonviolence

Alternatives to Violence Project / New England

Awards this Certificate to

Davon McNeil

Who has satisfactorily completed the Advanced Course in Nonviolent Conflict Resolution

Jazzy June — 4/3/11

Facilitators — Date

The Alternatives to Violence Program (AVP) workshops are amazing. I took this advanced workshop because I wanted to honestly discover what my internal triggers were/are. I learned that danger-spotting is a very useful tool in not being triggered; consisting of recognizing, in any situation, the things which could stimulate the habit-self towards drug usage, violence, or other destructive actions. Also, I learned the importance of humanizing and communicating to another person's inner-self from my own to defuse a tense situation where criminal-addictive thinking seems to be in charge.

Emotional Awareness Program

Certificate of Achievement

Awarded to

Davon McNeil

Has successfully completed a ten session course in

Emotional Awareness / Emotional Healing based upon the Houses of Healing by

Robin Casarjian

MCI Shirley — Dept of Correction Institution

Volunteer Facilitator

April 2011 — Date

The Emotional Awareness Program is a beautiful experience that provides what I like to call "strength through sensitivity." It is a therapeutic program within a circle of trust and integrity that helps men to understand the nature of emotions, the relationship between emotions and addiction, and emotional logic. It stresses the importance of being in tune with your emotions which was a huge wakeup call/lesson for me. We've dealt with other great topics such as trauma, impulse, empathy and emotions' influence on decision-making.

This program helped me to come to a greater sense of self and internal balance. Through facilitated discussions around different times and events in my life, I was rewarded with a better ability to perceive, balance and heal myself. I learned to communicate with others about my emotions and make better decisions in my life. This program has taught me how to channel my impulses, thoughts and emotions productively.

Menswork Program

The Menswork Program was and is a wonderful program. I learned a great deal about myself and how my father's absence in my life played a huge role in the choices I made while growing up. I learned that if I didn't do the necessary work in order to heal my wounded inner- child my life would become contaminated by the oozing wounds that remain below the surface. Also, if there is pain inside of me and it isn't made conscious—that is, if I'm not aware of the pain or too scared or numb to honestly acknowledge it and meet it with compassion—then I'll find myself stuck in a life filled with unresolved pain.

I learned that doing the work of going back to my childhood suffering would help me deal with the past hurts and move on with greater self-respect, freedom and creative power. I really enjoyed this program.

Menswork Program
(1st Time Facilitator)

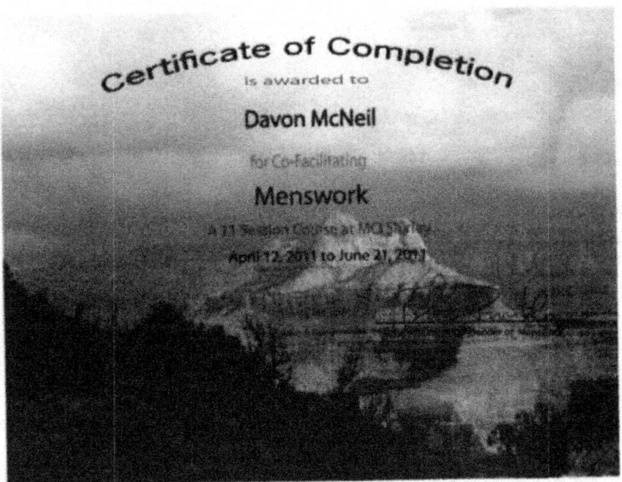

I joined the Menswork Program to help facilitate it. We had a large group of men striving to learn concepts of how to become real solid men. These men were determined to shed the negative thoughts which had kept them bound to childlike thinking, thus manifesting childlike behavior. We learned that it is the egotistical and hurt child's voice screaming out for attention which causes a lot of our destructive habits. Although these negative voices are always there, clamoring for our attention as we commit ourselves to knowing our cast of subpersonalities; honoring our feelings and listening more deeply to our true selves, we will find that inner peace, personal freedom and love that's rightfully ours.

Alternatives to Violence Project
(Forgiveness)

Alternatives to Violence Project
Shirley Medium Prison

This to certify that

Davan McNeil

Diligently attended and participated in an AVP Practice Group
Focusing on "*Forgiveness*"
April 25 - June 20, 2011

Jazzy June
Facilitator

Nurturing Neil
Facilitator

This Alternative to Violence Program (AVP) workshop was about "Forgiveness." I learned how to sincerely "forgive myself' with the tools and information provided within this workshop. These were two words (forgive myself) I needed to hear and feel and put into practice in my life, along with all the other therapeutic work, to feel settled inside of myself.

Self-forgiveness, like all healing, is a process. It's not a one-time event that happens overnight. I learned that self-forgiveness is highly individualistic. The first step to self-forgiveness is the act of acknowledging the truth; not only of what I've done, but also the truth about my inner feelings and the truth of how my actions have affected others. I learned a lot in this workshop.

The Father's Group

The Father's Group

CERTIFICATE OF COMPLETION

Davon McNeil W82395

July 13, 2011

For successfully completing an intensive twelve week course on the moral and legal responsibilities of fatherhood and effective parenting. Your voluntary involvement in the Father's Group, and proactive participation in our group discussions, planned parenting, and educational workshops helped to build a trusting, sharing, and learning atmosphere for all. As a graduate member of the Father's Group, you are now charged with the individual responsibility of continuing with the everyday learning process of fatherhood and the responsibility of being an effective parent.

Christine Brockelman, Director of Treatment

The Father's Group Program was very emotional for me because we spoke a lot about our children and how our coming to prison has affected them. Growing up without a father handicapped my ability to truly understand what a father's position is supposed to look like. I had my first child (daughter) at the age of fifteen years old. I was a child with a child.

This group allowed me to start the process of building a foundation to stand upon as it relates to honest fatherhood. I learned that the majority of incarcerated men unconsciously shut down their emotional attachment to their children while in prison because the experience and memories are extremely painful. We were instructed to write letters to our children—the age didn't matter—to apologize for leaving them in the world alone. This exercise helps to heal the pain which for me, helped a great deal.

Alternatives to Violence Project
(Patience and Inner Peace)

Alternatives to Violence Project
Shirley Medium Prison

This to certify that

Davon McNeil

Diligently attended and participated in an AVP Practice Group
Focusing on "Developing Core Self by Finding Patience and Inner Peace"
September 19 – November 14, 2011

Jazzy June
Facilitator

Nurturing Neil
Facilitator

This AVP workshop deals with "Developing Core Self by Finding Patience and Inner Peace." I learned that dependency on others for anything, especially happiness, is a slow, time- consuming process that we will never fully receive. True happiness comes from within one's self. Man/woman has the ability to learn without instructions or instructors, but we must have patience with ourselves. Also, everyone made a journey.

To establish patience and inner peace, we must try to understand where others are coming from. I learned to trust my inner sense of when to act and when to withdraw. The moment we define stress as coming from anywhere other than from within ourselves, we set ourselves up to experience it; we're too late to prevent it. The more we think about it or attempt to change it, the worse it will seem because we are validating that the stress exists outside of ourselves. This workshop was powerful.

Alternatives to Violence Project
(Facilitator Training)

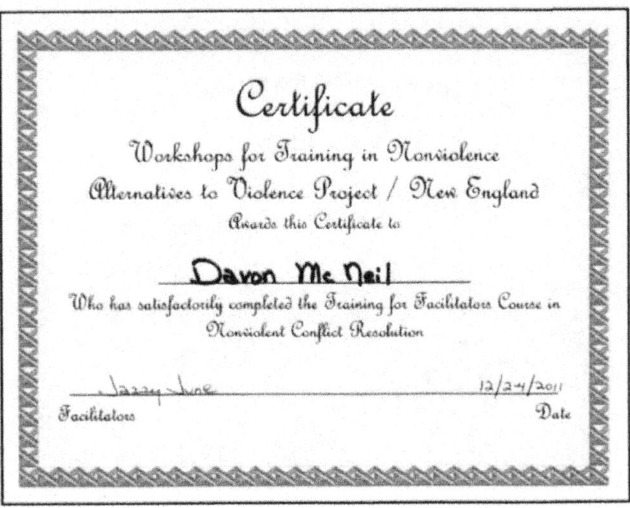

Certificate

Workshops for Training in Nonviolence

Alternatives to Violence Project / New England

Awards this Certificate to

Davon Mc Neil

Who has satisfactorily completed the Training for Facilitators Course in Nonviolent Conflict Resolution

12/24/2011

Facilitators | Date

I enrolled in this AVP workshop to become a facilitator within the program. There were many young men in this group who wanted to learn how to prevent themselves from committing acts of violence. This was a no-nonsense group of young men; the energy in the classroom was intense because the majority of us were incarcerated for murder. We all wanted to learn about ourselves and why we committed the crimes we were responsible for.

We learned to ask our inner-selves for a non-violent way because there's always one inside of us. When we're clear about our position, expect to experience great inward power to act on it. A response that relies on this power will be courageous and without hostility. I really enjoyed facilitating this workshop.

Menswork Program
(Facilitator Review)

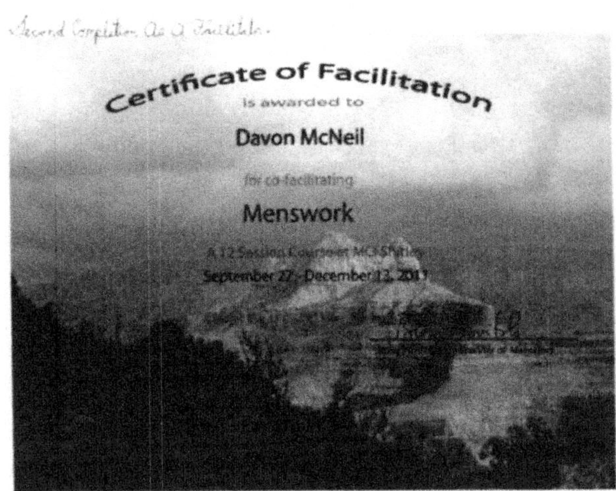

Certificate of Facilitation
is awarded to
Davon McNeil
for co-facilitating
Menswork

I was commissioned by the Menswork founder to join the group again as a facilitator for the second time. I had a wonderful experience facilitating this group. It made me feel good to know that the founder of the Menswork Program trusted in my ability to lead the group. We all learned a lot in this group.

I taught these men to take some time every week to do sky awareness (mental clearing) and reflect upon these questions: 1) Who am I? 2) Why am I here? 3) What can I do to better myself? 4) Why should I serve others? I explained to these men that these were some of the very questions that I had to ask myself to start the process of true change.

Responsible Fatherhood Program

Responsible Fatherhood Program

A collaborative program of the Massachusetts Department of Correction & Spectrum Health Systems, Inc

Certificate of Completion

This certificate is awarded to

Davon McNeil

for successfully completing the Responsible Fatherhood Program

Admission date 11/15/11 Completion date 1/6/12

Responsible Fatherhood Program Counselor

Director of Treatment

I wanted to attend a fatherhood class (Responsible Fatherhood Program) for a second time because my maturity level had risen since the initial Father's Group Program. Also, I was now seeing and speaking with my two daughters on a consistent basis. This allowed me to clearly understand the importance of being a father.

I learned that it doesn't matter where I am physically. My duty and responsibility as a father still remains the same. My daughters forgave me for my absence and simply want me to hurry up and come home (smile). There's nothing better than my daughters telling me they love me no matter what I've done because everyone has a past; even saints.

DAVON MCNEIL

Alternatives to Violence Project
(Apprenticeship Training for Active Facilitators)

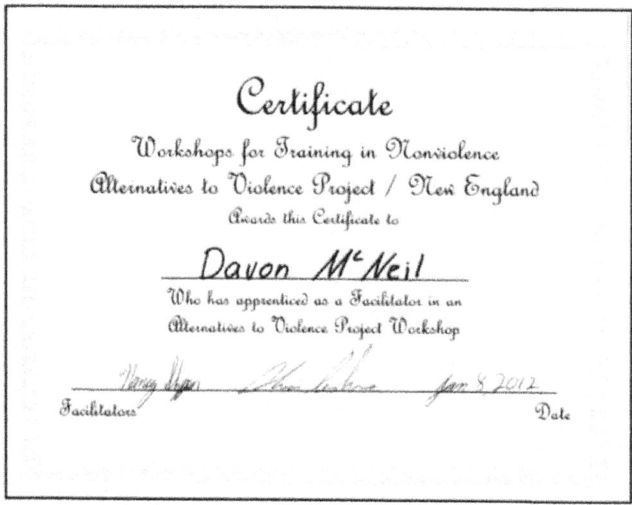

Certificate

Workshops for Training in Nonviolence

Alternatives to Violence Project / New England

Awards this Certificate to

Davon McNeil

Who has apprenticed as a Facilitator in an Alternatives to Violence Project Workshop

Jan 8 2012

Facilitators Date

I went through my apprenticeship training to become an active facilitator within the Alternatives to Violence Program (AVP) workshops. I learned that transforming power is within every person. We can find it in ourselves, recognize it in others and grow more skillful in opening ourselves to its use.

We seek to be assertive—not passive or aggressive—in addressing our own real needs and the injustice we see around us. Each of us searches for a path of non-violence and we welcome all seekers, regardless if they appear before or behind us on the path. By working together, we learn from one another the valuable things each one of us have to offer. We also prevent one another from straying too far from the path of non-violence. I really learned a lot about myself during this workshop.

Alternatives to Violence Project (Family Life From Behind the Wire)

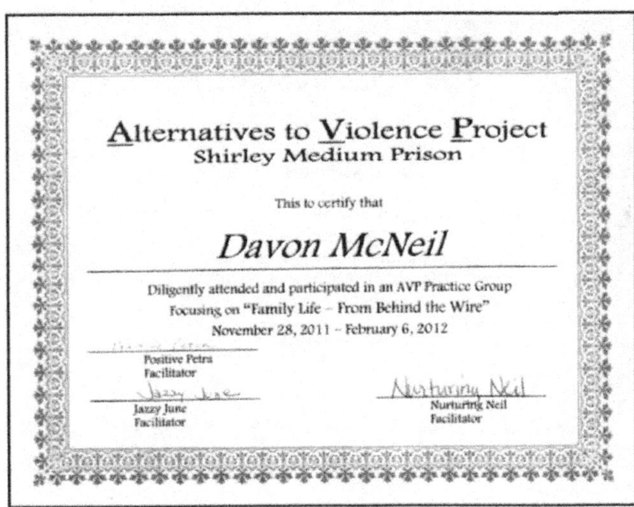

Alternatives to Violence Project
Shirley Medium Prison

This to certify that

Davon McNeil

Diligently attended and participated in an AVP Practice Group
Focusing on "Family Life - From Behind the Wire"
November 28, 2011 - February 6, 2012

Positive Petra
Facilitator

Jazzy June
Facilitator

Nurturing Neil
Facilitator

This Alternatives to Violence Project (AVP) was centered around "Family Life From Behind the Wire." We discussed the effects of our crimes and how they (crimes) impacted our families, communities, other families, the victim's families and innocent members of society.

I learned that most crimes happen quickly; and usually just as quickly we flee the crime scene. Its rip and run, beat 'em and beat it. Maybe we only remember frightened faces, or maybe much more, or much worse. But few of us, whether our crimes were against people and/or property, think much about the suffering which we leave in our wake with each and every crime that we commit.

Yes, of course, most of us who have committed crimes have painful lives too, and we know that our families and victims suffer. But neither fact is the same thing as facing up to how much pain we've caused. And there can be no room for doubt that the person who caused the pain is the same person who committed the crime (us). The suffering didn't "just happen." We can be responsible for something even if we didn't plan it or want it. If you've never thought about that idea before, please do.

The Four Agreements Program

The Four Agreements

CERTIFICATE OF COMPLETION

Davon McNeil W-82395

October 17, 2012

This certificate is awarded for the participation and successful completion of The Four Agreements Program

Director of Treatment

The Four Agreements Program was a very spiritual experience for me. It seemed as if though each of the four concepts were spoken to me in the past by my grandmother who had passed away years before I participated in this program. The fourth agreement, "Always Do Your Best," contain words of divine wisdom that my grandmother would share with me when I was growing up.

I learned that my best will change from moment-to-moment; it will be different when I'm healthy as opposed to sick. No matter the circumstances, I must simply do my best and I will avoid self-judgment, self-abuse and regret. I learned that how I treat others is a direct result of how I feel about myself.

Also, I learned that every aspect of my life grows richer as I give thanks for what I already have and what is yet to come. We need to understand and appreciate the past for what it can teach us about living more in the now. Understand that right now, this very moment, is where life is truly lived.

Four Agreements Program
(Review)

The Four Agreements

CERTIFICATE OF COMPLETION

Davon NcNeil W-82395

November 28, 2012

This certificate is awarded for the participation
and successful completion of The Four Agreements Program

Deputy Superintendent

It was very important for me to attend this program for a second time. I benefited greatly from this program and the training in meditation that it provided. It helped me to conceive forgiveness better, through awareness that everything, no matter how good or bad, happened in my life due to a chain of events that influenced my actions.

I learned not to take anything personally; nothing others do is because of me. What others say and do is a projection of their own reality; their own dream. When I am immune to the opinions and actions of others, I won't be the victim of needless suffering. Also, I learned to take some time every day to be silent and go inward. This program taught me the value of listening to the wisdom of my own heart.

Alternatives to Violence Project
(How to Handle Anger)

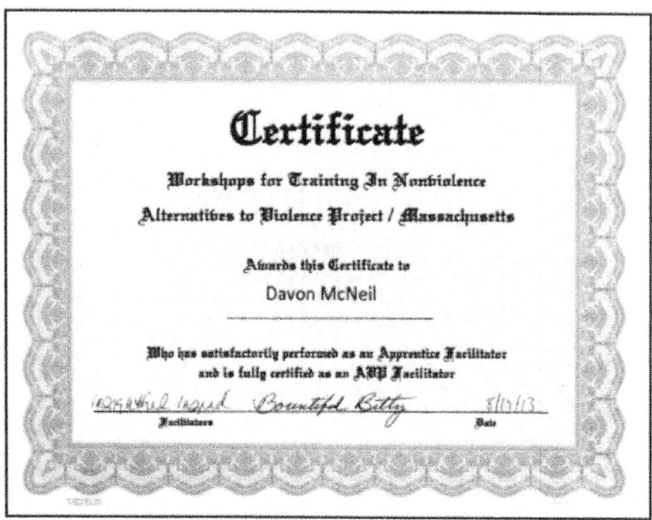

Certificate

Workshops for Training In Nonviolence

Alternatives to Violence Project / Massachusetts

Awards this Certificate to

Davon McNeil

Who has satisfactorily performed as an Apprentice Facilitator
and is fully certified as an AVP Facilitator

Facilitators

Date

I wanted to truly internalize the lessons that I've learned within the Alternatives to Violence Program (AVP) workshops. Therefore, I've attended this program numerous times. What I've learned in this particular workshop is that how I was treated while growing up, and what I learned from others about how to handle anger, has a profound impact on how I deal with my anger today. Also, we see what we see based upon our mental conditioning and beliefs (our thought system).

I learned that the mind and the physical brain are not one and the same. The mind is the source of all unworldly insight, which is transmitted through the brain, which expresses the information by way of the tongue (the verbal delivery organ).

Alternatives to Violence Project
(Recovery)

Certificate

Workshops for Training in Nonviolence

Alternatives to Violence Project / Massachusetts

Awards this Certificate to

Davon McNeil

Who has been a Facilitator team member in a Workshop in Nonviolent Conflict Resolution

Bountiful Betty — Aug. 17, 2013

Facilitators — Date

This AVP (Alternatives to Violence Program) workshop was centered on "Recovery." The recovery slogan, "One day at a time," reminds us that we make progress best if we just take things step-by-step carefully and don't worry over what lies down the road.

I learned that crime and suffering has caused a lot of us men in prison to simply give up hope, but incarceration offers us a rare opportunity to set a new course for our lives. As we begin to define our goals for the near future and beyond, think about the following: Do your goals lead in safe directions? Are your goals consistent with each other? Are your current activities leading towards your goals?

We're striving to avoid negative and violent situations at all cost. Therefore, we have to remain laser-focused on our recovery. It doesn't matter if we're recovering from drugs or criminal-addictive thinking, we've got to correct the content of our character. I've learned that no matter the consequences, those who are honest with themselves get further in life.

Alternatives to Violence Project (Perception–Facilitator Training)

Certificate

Workshops for Training in Nonviolence

Alternatives to Violence Project / Massachusetts

Awards this Certificate to

Davon McNeil

Who has been a Facilitator team member in a Workshop in Nonviolent Conflict Resolution

Facilitators Date

I attended this AVP (Alternatives to Violence Program) workshop to remain structured and focused on the lessons I've learned by attending and facilitating these workshops. I made a conscious choice to change my life for the better, so I'm constantly involving myself in positive programs/workshops.

I learned that my own thoughts and attitudes about a particular person, place or thing is the cause of my feelings and actions. I also learned that perception is very important for our wellbeing; for our peace. Perception should be free from emotion, ignorance and illusions.

As you become happier you enter a new dimension of life which plant seeds for further spiritual growth. The present moment is where we find true happiness and inner peace. These AVP workshops have allowed me to transcend into a higher realm of harmony.

Alternatives to Violence Project
(Facilitator Renewal)

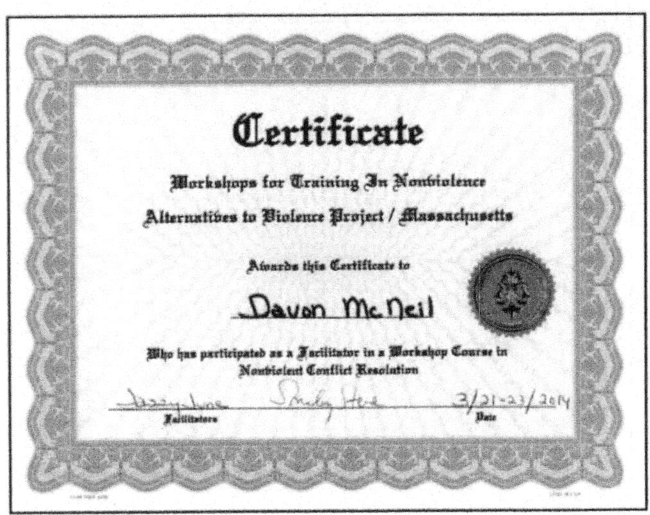

Certificate

Workshops for Training In Nonviolence

Alternatives to Violence Project / Massachusetts

Awards this Certificate to

Davon McNeil

Who has participated as a Facilitator in a Workshop Course in Nonviolent Conflict Resolution

3/21-23/2014

Facilitators | Date

This AVP (Alternatives to Violence Program) workshop was a refresher and renewal class for all of us who had facilitated in prior workshops. We went over a lot of the key terms and concepts of the program: 1) Correctional - learning to correct behaviors and incorrect ideas; 2) Recovery - an ongoing process that involves both abstinence from drugs/alcohol as well as changes in areas of life-functioning; 3) Criminality - the tendency to break the law in order to satisfy your own desires or impulses; and 4) Habit-Self - the part of you ruled by habits. Habit- Self doesn't think; just reacts on feelings and memory. Habit-Self needs to be restrained so that its grip is loosened and it no longer controls your entire life.

The above are some of the key terms and concepts that are taught within the AVP workshops. These key terms and concepts have literally helped me to change my life from negative to positive. But these key terms and concepts have to be sealed in one's heart to be effective in reality. Deliberate awareness is the order of the day for me. You get out of AVP what you put into AVP.

Alternatives to Violence Project
(Criminally-Addictive Behavior Disorder)

Certificate

Workshops for Training in Nonviolence

Alternatives to Violence Project / Massachusetts

Awards this Certificate to

Davon McNeil

Who has been a Facilitator team member in a Workshop in

Nonviolent Conflict Resolution

Facilitators Date

This AVP (Alternatives to Violence Program) workshop was another renewal process for me and a few facilitators. We went over a few of the disorders that a lot of us men suffer from in prison and are striving to overcome by involving ourselves within these workshops/programs.

The criminal-addictive lifestyle is viewed as a disorder of the whole person involving some or all of the areas of functioning. While the conduct, attitude and thinking of an individual may be wrong or "bad," the inner person is fundamentally good. In the recovery and change process, when a person is nurtured, understood and accepted by others, that inner person can emerge. Many persons living a criminal lifestyle or substance abuse lifestyle connect their inner person with their bad behavior.

I will always be humbled by the teachings of the AVP. I know many great men who will never see the free world again because of a mistake they made 20, 30 or even 40 years ago. However, these men utilized the AVP workshops to ultimately change their lives.

Blood Spill/Sewage Clean-Up Program

BLOOD SPILL/SEWAGE CLEAN UP PROGRAM

CERTIFICATE OF COMPLETION

This certificate is awarded to: McNEIL NAVON # W82395
(Inmate/Patient Name and Number)

Who in accordance with the DOC 450 Inmate Work Assignment policy successfully completed the Blood Spill/Sewage Clean Up Review Program as of 10-21-14
(Date)

Norbert Melo
Environmental Health and Safety Officer

Martha Chapman IPN
Infection Control Nurse

I will never get used to cleaning up blood and feces. But it's a very humbling experience. I learned about many particles which exist in the atmosphere during a blood or feces clean-up. I also learned about the dangers of exposure to airborne bacteria and spreading contamination. Please understand and know that there is a correct way to clean up blood and feces. If you don't know...learn!

High School Equivalency Credential (GED)

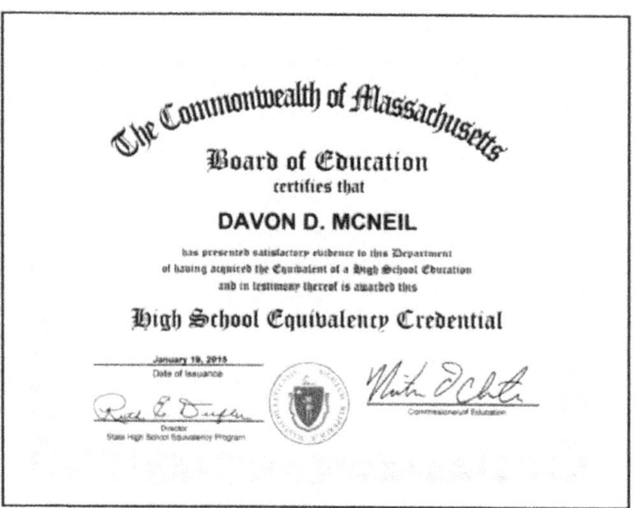
The Commonwealth of Massachusetts
Board of Education
certifies that
DAVON D. MCNEIL
has presented satisfactory evidence to this Department
of having acquired the Equivalent of a High School Education
and in testimony thereof is awarded this
High School Equivalency Credential

January 19, 2015
Date of Issuance

Director
State High School Equivalency Program

Commissioner of Education

I always frowned upon going to school. I was mentally conditioned to believe that going to school was for suckers. It seemed as if though all the cool and popular guys were getting their education in the streets. Therefore, that's where I went to get mine (education). Well, guess what? When I entered the prison system, I found all of the cool and popular guys who chose to get their education in the streets, sitting in a prison cell.

We graduated with high honors from the streets and were accepted into the state prison system. I formed deep bonds with men who were sentenced to spend the rest of their natural lives in prison. These men became my mentors and encouraged me to turn my prison experience into a learning experience. Many of these men had acquired college degrees and were teaching us younger men the importance of having an education.

I was determined to get my GED (General Educational Development) credential and I achieved my goal. It took extreme patience and discipline, but it was well worth it. I want to thank all of my mentors who guided me along my path to manifesting my reality.

GED Congratulations Certificate

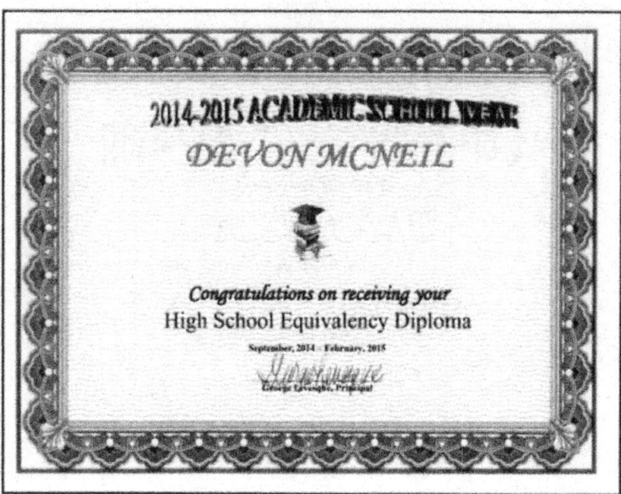

I received this certificate prior to my graduation. It felt really good knowing that my hard work had paid off. I have to thank my many mentors who pushed and inspired me to seek education while incarcerated. Thank you very much.

Basic Computer Skills

Certificate of Participation

is hereby awarded to

DAVON MCNEIL

for Participating in the

Computer Skills - Basic

February, 2015 - June, 2015

I know and understand that technology has advanced the world. I felt it was, and still is, my duty and responsibility to take full advantage of the basic computer skills class to obtain an understanding of how to operate a computer after being incarcerated for sixteen years. I had a lot of fun learning how to utilize both of my hands to work the keyboard. It was amazing to see and learn about all the features of Microsoft's Word software. I look forward to becoming more computer-literate upon my release from prison by enrolling in advanced computer classes.

Certificate of Participation
(Talent Show)

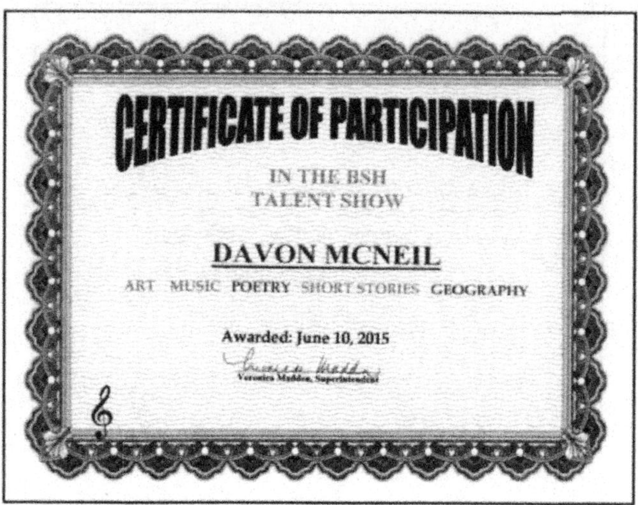
CERTIFICATE OF PARTICIPATION

IN THE BSH
TALENT SHOW

DAVON MCNEIL

ART MUSIC POETRY SHORT STORIES GEOGRAPHY

Awarded: June 10, 2015

Veronica Madden, Superintendent

I've learned to channel my anger and express my emotions in a positive and constructive manner. Poetry has given me an outlet to share my inner feelings and thoughts with the world. When I'm sitting alone within this 8'xlO' cell. I'm able to reflect on my past life within that ominous, negative culture (the streets) and tap into my deeper self. The fire which rests at my lower spinal cord begins to ignite and words of intense heat scorch the lined paper lying in front of me:

My past will not define me.

Bars cannot confine me.

I am not my dark flesh, which is weak.

I exist as infinite intelligence.

I am the essence of repentance.

DAVON MCNEIL

Assertive Communication Workshop

Commonwealth of Massachusetts
Department of Correction

Certificate of Achievement
awarded to:

Davon McNeil W82395

for having successfully completed the 4- hour
Assertive Communication Workshop
attended on 5/7/15 and 5/14/15

Director of Treatment

5/14/15
Date

I learned that assertive communication is very helpful in many areas of my life. Growing up in the negative culture of street life, I lacked the ability to communicate effectively. This program taught me how to ask for what I want without sounding aggressive or demanding. Also, I learned to speak up for myself when I know that something is not right or I feel uncomfortable.

This program taught me how to communicate effectively during a job interview and when I'm in the presence of authority figures. Assertive communication will establish our boundaries and allow others to know exactly what we are saying to them. I learned that there is nothing wrong with saying, "No," especially to my two daughters (smile).

Active Listening Workshop

Commonwealth of Massachusetts
Department of Correction

Certificate of Achievement
awarded to:

Davon McNeil, W-82395

For having successfully completed the 4- hour
Active Listening Workshop
Attended on 5/28/15, 6/4/15
dates

Director of Treatment

Program Facilitator(s)

6/4/15
Date

Listening is a skill that is extremely important because our attention span in today's society is very limited. For many years I only heard what I wanted to hear. Active listening is a key ingredient when we're angry or frustrated. We tend to shut all reasoning down and only hear negative self-talk or words coming from the person we've allowed to get inside our head, causing the anger or frustration. Focusing will allow us to pull our attention and energy back into active listening when we seem to wander.

Problem-Solving Workshop

Commonwealth of Massachusetts
Department of Correction

Certificate of Achievement
awarded to:

Davon Mcneil

for having successfully completed the 4- hour
Problem Solving Workshop
attended on 6/11/15 & 6/18/15

Director of Treatment — Program Facilitator

6/18/15
Date

I learned that problems are only situations that we've yet to figure out. Some problems are greater than others and need to be paid close attention because they can be life-altering whether good or bad. We must be able to do self-listening: being able to hear and understand our own thoughts; and knowing whether they are coming from our habit-self or inner-self. I've experienced my share of problems while incarcerated and thankfully, my ability to problem- solve and communicate were readily available to me.

I've learned to utilize "calming" as a tool for problem-solving. Calming is an on-the-spot technique which involves mindful breathing and utilizing "I" statements such as, "I am not going to get upset," or "I have a bright future ahead of me." I am not saying that problem-solving is easy, but it can be done if you're really striving to grow into a better individual.

Negotiation Workshop

Commonwealth of Massachusetts
Department of Correction

Certificate of Achievement
awarded to:

Devon McNeil, W-82395

for having successfully completed the 4- hour
Negotiating Workshop
attended on

Director of Treatment   Kaitlin Mullen Shot Poole Mith
Program Facilitator

7/2/15
Date

This was a fun program. I learned the art of negotiation to accomplish many things in life. Negotiating allows you to exercise your mental muscles; putting to use all that you've learned from your life's experiences. But I've learned that negotiating must be founded upon positive intention. We should never strive to get something for nothing or by deception. We will not always be successful in our negotiations but we should always strive to learn a lesson from negotiating with others. We performed a lot of role play to demonstrate effective negotiating which made the program entertaining while learning.

Asking For Help Workshop

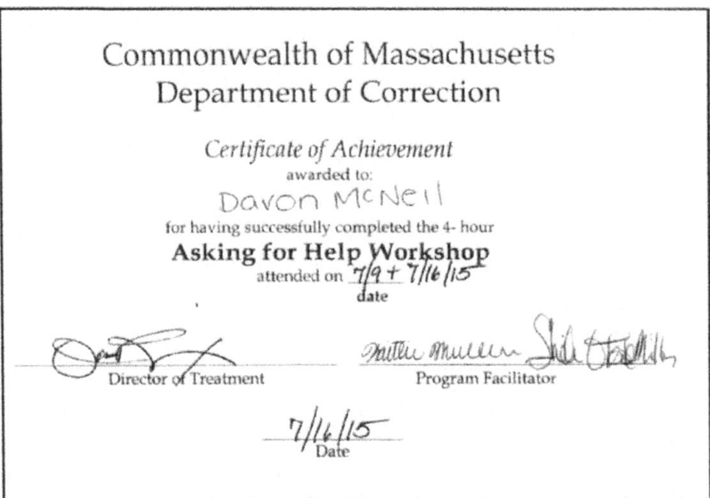
Commonwealth of Massachusetts
Department of Correction

Certificate of Achievement
awarded to:
Davon McNeil
for having successfully completed the 4- hour
Asking for Help Workshop
attended on 7/9 + 7/16/15
date

Director of Treatment

Program Facilitator

7/16/15
Date

I've always had an issue with asking for help. But I learned the value of asking others for help. I learned that a lot of men in prison suffer from being let down on an extremely consistent basis. Therefore, we've conditioned ourselves to never ask for help which has caused many of us to commit thoughtless harm to others and ourselves. I've learned to do away with the negative aspects of the ego, pride and "I can do it myself' attitude. There is no success without the help of other people. Asking for help makes navigating through life a lot easier.

Use of Self-Control Workshop

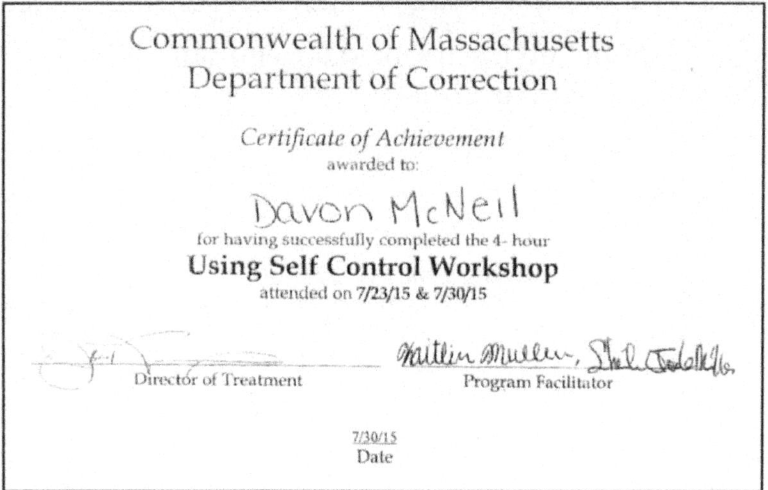
Commonwealth of Massachusetts
Department of Correction

Certificate of Achievement
awarded to:

Davon McNeil

for having successfully completed the 4- hour
Using Self Control Workshop
attended on **7/23/15 & 7/30/15**

Director of Treatment

Program Facilitator

7/30/15
Date

This was a good program, although, a lot of the information I learned in previous programs. But I did learn the science of keeping written records of my feelings which I experienced throughout the day. Once I began recording my feelings I learned a lot about myself and some of my emotional triggers. Whether an individual is incarcerated or in society, your self-control must be activated at all times.

Setting Goals Workshop

Commonwealth of Massachusetts
Department of Correction

Certificate of Achievement
awarded to:

Davon McNeil

for having successfully completed the 4- hour

Setting Goals Workshop

attended on 8/6/15 & 8/13/15

Director of Treatment

Program Facilitator

8/13/15

To be successful in life, we must set goals for ourselves. I learned to set small goals and then start the process of achieving them; slowly and steadily. Many of us who have spent a significant amount of time in prison tend to set these grandiose goals for our lives after incarceration, negating the fact that we've spent decades in prison. Our intentions are positive, but we fail to realize the concept of, "one day at a time." And when these huge goals aren't achieved, we allow the emotion of failure to rule us, thus setting in motion the habit-self way of thinking (our old habits of getting what we want). We find ourselves back in prison, mad at everyone except the man in the mirror who neglected to, first, set smaller goals.

Violence Reduction Program

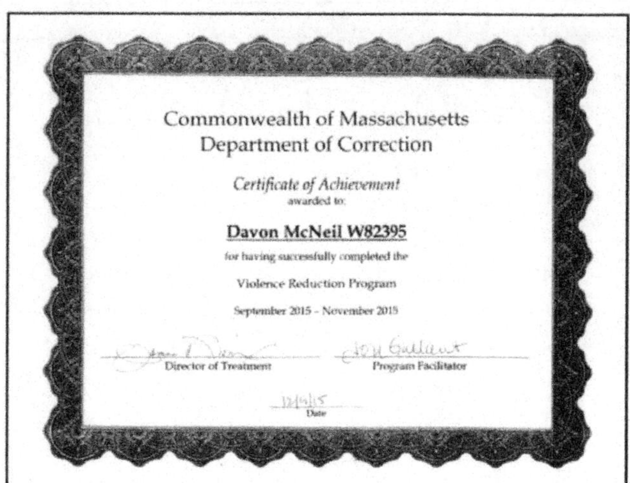

Commonwealth of Massachusetts
Department of Correction

Certificate of Achievement
awarded to:

Davon McNeil W82395

for having successfully completed the

Violence Reduction Program

September 2015 - November 2015

Director of Treatment — Program Facilitator

12/4/15
Date

The Violence Reduction Program was a very serious learning experience for me. We worked as a team in order to creatively come up with ways and opportunities for building a nonviolent future. I learned to pause and give myself time to think before reacting. We have to turn the emotion of anger into passion in the pursuit of better ideals such as goals of positive growth, academic excellence, social advancement and brotherhood. The above will assist in helping us to focus on a non-violent path.

I learned that when we're hurt on a consistent basis as children, we learn how to numb our feelings. It's a natural reaction. It can become our only protection against suffering. The numbness towards our pain then manifests into the numbness towards the pain of others as well. This numbness can manifest as passive indifference to the sufferings of others or, in its extreme, it becomes active cruelty. It is this numbness to your own pain that is at the core of much of what is considered evil and lands us in prison.

Also, I learned the pain may lie hidden under years and layers of numbness. We may have had to become indifferent to our pain to survive. If this is the case, to heal, we must gently and with great compassion now peel away the layers of numbness and indifference to ourselves. It's a must!

Countdown to Freedom Program

Countdown to Freedom

An eight week program that prepares men to leave prison with an openness to new ways of thinking and with the skills necessary to find employment and create healthy lifestyles.

Davon McNeil

Has successfully completed Countdown to Freedom

Lindsey Wass, LICSW — Chaplain Peg Newman, BCC, MEd — Date

The Countdown to Freedom Program was very insightful for me because it taught me a lot about what to expect once I'm granted my physical freedom. We watched a video about men who had served time in prison and were now in society living productive lives. Each of these men shared their story regarding the struggles they experienced upon their release from prison.

I learned that attitude adjustment is very important to integrate successfully back into society. Many of us who have spent a decade or more in prison have conditioned ourselves to the everyday routine of surviving within an extremely hostile environment. Therefore, our attitudes are frozen into alertness; always suspicious and on edge.

I also learned the science of operating from my inner-self on a consistent basis. The inner-self is the part of you which is responsible, thoughtful and reasonable. We all have an inner-self. The inner-self does not get triggered into aggression or defensiveness like the habit- self. I've learned to strengthen my inner-self because it's the part of me that can learn and restrain my habit-self.

Restorative Justice

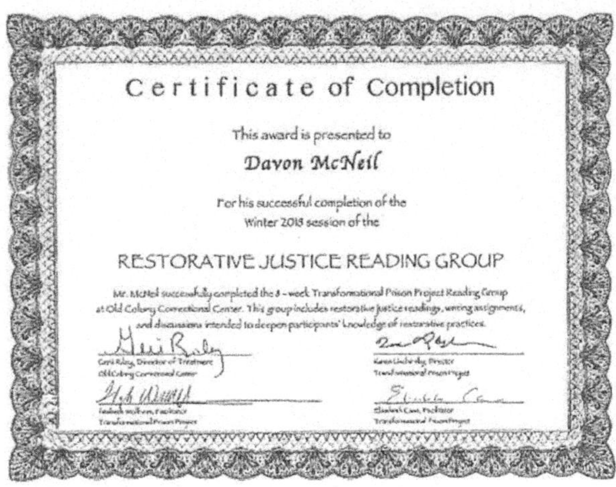

Certificate of Completion

This award is presented to

Davon McNeil

For his successful completion of the
Winter 2018 session of the

RESTORATIVE JUSTICE READING GROUP

Mr. McNeil successfully completed the 8-week Transformational Prison Project Reading Group at Old Colony Correctional Center. This group includes restorative justice readings, writing assignments, and discussions intended to deepen participants' knowledge of restorative practices.

Director of Treatment, Old Colony Correctional Center

Director, Transformational Prison Project

Facilitator, Transformational Prison Project

Facilitator, Transformational Prison Project

This program is one of the best programs that I've participated in during my 19 years of incarceration. I've thought long and hard about my crime, the victim and the victim's family. I learned that my crime has a never-ending ripple effect that has harmed many people, even generations. Also, I learned that restorative justice is a process which involves, to the extent possible, those who have a stake in a specific offense; and to collectively identify and address harms, needs and obligations in order to heal and make things as right as possible. We were exposed to some very enlightening concepts such as focusing on the harms of crime rather than the rules that have been broken; showing equal concern and commitment to victims and offenders while involving both in the process of justice; and lastly, providing opportunities for dialogue, direct or indirect, between victims and offenders as appropriate. As a society, we need to really give restorative justice some serious thought.

DAVON MCNEIL

Companion Program

Companion Program

New Companion Training Program

Davon McNeil

has successfully completed a comprehensive training program designed to prepare individuals to work with men who have a mental illness ~ June 14, 2017

Denise McDonough, Deputy Superintendent
Peg Newman, BCC, M.Ed.
Allison Howland, LMHC, PCC

I was selected to participate in the Companion Program after being interviewed by a panel of four Massachusetts Department of Corrections staff members. Prior to my participation in the program, I was completely ignorant and bad absolutely no understanding of mental illness. After six months of being involved in the program, I was assigned a companion by the name of Mr. Marcus Guest. He was 74 years old and bad been in prison approximately 45 years at the time of our introduction. Mr. Guest was confined to a wheelchair as a result of suffering a stroke, but his mind was still as sharp as a tack (when he wanted it to be). Mr. Guest was diagnosed with severe paranoid schizophrenia and manic depression. He loved to sing old blues songs and would sing to me for hours while sitting in the small recreation yard situated off of the housing unit. He and I formed a bond and became really close to the point that we looked forward to each other's company. I learned a lot from him as he shared his life story and experiences with me. He would always say to me, "Young man, you have to treat life like a beautiful woman — be patient with it and always treat it with the utmost respect!" I truly miss my friend, Mr. Marcus Guest.

Able Minds Program

Bridgewater State Hospital
Library Services

A.B.L.E. M.I.N.D.S.
Using Literature to Transform Behavior

This Certificate is presented to

Davon McNeil

In recognition of your participation in the 8-week

ABLE MINDS
Consequential Thinking Seminar

Kurt W. Eichner, Instructor

SEPTEMBER 21, 2016
Date

This was an interesting program. It was centered on utilizing literature in order to transform our thinking and behavior. We read a few short stories and then broke out into groups to discuss what we learned from each story and how the stories directly or indirectly related to our lives. In my opinion the story selections could have been better, but I really enjoyed the group discussions. I tend to learn more about me while listening to others share their stories.

Health Awareness (2018)

Certificate of Completion
Awarded to:
Davon McNeil
For your Presentation @
Old Colony Correctional Center
Health Awareness Program
May 2018
HIV Test Counselor & Educator, Tracy Horton
HIV/HCV Admin Manager, Claudia Gonzalez

I took this program a second time as a refresher because it was very informative. However, retaining all of the information was very hard so this time I brought a notebook with me. This particular class was centered on the immune system. How do you begin to compromise the immune system?

Drinking and drugging.

Alcohol and cocaine have direct effects on T4 cell production.

Poor nutrition — no one stays healthy without proper nutrition.

Negative thinking - will drag you down mentally, physically and spiritually.

Too much stress - there's growing evidence that too much stress wears out the body.

Too little sleep.

What kinds of activities enhance or improve the immune system?

Sobriety

Exercise

Relaxation

Good Nutrition

Meditation

Positive Thinking (my favorite)

Journal Writing

Anger Management – SAMHSA Program

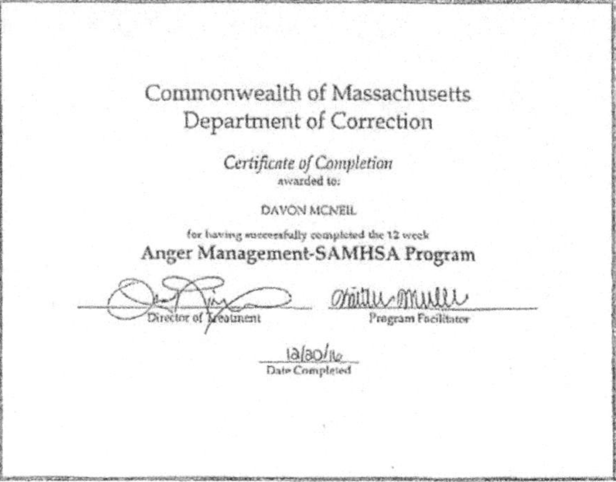

Commonwealth of Massachusetts
Department of Correction

Certificate of Completion
awarded to:

DAVON MCNEIL

for having successfully completed the 12 week
Anger Management-SAMHSA Program

Director of Treatment — Program Facilitator

12/30/16
Date Completed

One of the main topics of this program was unresolved anger. I learned that unresolved anger is one of the chief contributing factors to the destruction of marriages, the breakdown of families and the weakening of communities. It's also a major cause of health problems, a lack of productivity in the workplace and a common denominator among juvenile delinquents. The program examined, what is the root cause of anger? The root cause of anger is tensions from past hurts and guilt I learned that this mixture of pain and guilt is cumulative and erupts into anger when new offenses remind us of hurtful past experiences. Most people assume that hurtful events from the past will be forgotten and will have no effect on the future. But that's not true. Past hurts do not just go away, nor does guilt simply disappear after a wrong response to a situation. Unless these experiences are resolved through repentance and forgiveness, we will continue to experience bouts of anger when our tension-points are triggered. This was a great program. I really learned a lot about my past and how anger played a huge role in my current situation.

DAVON MCNEIL

Nurturing Fathers Program

Certificate of Achievement

This certifies that

DEVON MCNEIL

has successfully completed

THE NURTURING FATHERS PROGRAM

AS PART OF THE 2017 READ TO ME FATHER PROGRAM

This program really helped me to understand how important it is for men in prison to remain in contact with their children. Most men in prison give up on trying to maintain contact with their children because so many barriers are placed before them: a child's unwilling mother, the courts, prison restrictions and plain laziness and irresponsibility on the prisoner's part During my 19 years of incarceration I've always strived to nurture my two daughters through phone calls, letters and visits. It wasn't always easy but I never gave up hope. I'm honestly proud to mention that my oldest daughter has graduated horn college and my youngest daughter is currently in college. Both of my babies will tell anyone about the bond that we share and the divine knowledge, wisdom and understanding that I've blessed them with over the years which kept them nurtured. Never allow prison to prevent you from being a nurturing father.

Breaking Barriers

Certificate of Participation

This certificate is awarded to:

Davon McNeil

for excellent group participation in

Breaking Barriers

August 9, 2016
Bridgewater State Hospital

Ms. Brooks, M.A.
Doctoral Psychology Intern
Group Facilitator

I really appreciate what I have learned in this program. I've come to know that long-held self-destructive behaviors, attitudes and self-images involve struggle and even suffering. Becoming personally "fit" in the Breaking Barriers program is equal to becoming physically "fit." Developing physical strength, losing weight, increasing stamina and endurance requires focus, effort, discipline, sacrifice, tiring workouts and boring practice. But mainly it involves aches, pain and sometimes fear associated with stretching beyond previous limits. The acceptance of pain as criteria for growth is important for members who have avoided discomfort in its various forms. Seek the courage to change!

Peer Educator (Health Awareness)

Certificate of Completion

Awarded to:

Davon McNeil

For completing the 12 week
Old Colony Correctional Center
Peer Educator Program
March , 2018

HIV/HCV Counselor & Educator, Tracy Horton

HIV/HCV Admin. Manager, Claudia Gonzalez

I was selected to participate in the Health Awareness Program as a peer educator. My responsibility was to help educate the new members about the importance of maintaining health awareness. I was instructed to teach on the subject of needle sharing. The most effective way for someone who uses hypodermic needles and syringes to avoid contracting HTV is to not share their injection equipment. If needles and syringes are to be shared, the following are some simple recommendations for sterilizing injection equipment:

Step 1. Fill the syringe to the top with fresh, clean water. Once the syringe is filled with water, shake and tap the syringe. Eject the water in the syringe away from where the "cooker" (a spoon or a bottle cap), water and bleach are situated, flushing out all of its contents. Perform this step three (3) times.

Step 2. Fill the syringe to the top with 100% full strength, liquid household bleach. Once the syringe is filled with bleach, shake and tap the syringe. Eject the bleach from the syringe away from where the "cooker," water and bleach are situated, flushing out all of its contents. Perform this step three (3) times.

Step 3. Fill the syringe to the top with new, clean water. Once the syringe is filled with water, shake and tap the syringe. Eject the water from the syringe away from where the "cooker,"

water and bleach are situated, flushing out all its contents. Perform this step three (3) times.

Warning:

It is very dangerous to inject bleach into the bloodstream. Cleaning the needle and syringe in this way does not insure that there will not be transmission of HIV, but it reduces the chances by a significant amount. When injecting substances that have been cooked and made into liquid form, the cooker also needs to be disinfected with bleach and rinsed with water. The filtering material should be disposed of after one use because it may be contaminated with blood, and there is not a complete way to disinfect it.

Restorative Justice (Circle Keeper)

CERTIFICATE OF COMPLETION

Second Time
THIS CIRCLE KEEPER'S CERTIFICATE
IS AWARDED TO

Davon McNeil

THIS 26 DAY OF March, 2019
IN RECOGNITION OF LEADERSHIP IN THE

RESTORATIVE JUSTICE READING GROUP

THIS GROUP INCLUDES RESTORATIVE JUSTICE READINGS, WRITING ASSIGNMENTS AND DISCUSSIONS INTENDED TO DEEPEN PARTICIPANTS' KNOWLEDGE OF RESTORATIVE PRACTICES.

I was selected to return to the Restorative Justice program as a circle keeper. As a circle keeper it was my responsibility to help the new members of the circle feel comfortable about talking in the group. Also, I explained exactly what the program was about and my past experiences while participating in the program for the very first time. The circle brings together all justice participants, including members of the broader community, to speak about crime and its effects. While seated in a circle, each participant talks about why they're participating. The circle members then create a plan for the offending members to make amends to the victim and community as well as address the causes of the crime. I really enjoyed helping other men open up about their past. We're all on the healing path.

Health Awareness

Certificate of Completion
Awarded to:
Davon McNeil
For completing the 7 Week
Old Colony Correctional Center
Health Awareness Education Program
November 2017

HIV Counselor & Educator, Tracy Horton
HIV/HCV Admin. Manager, Claudia Gonzalez

This program taught me many important things about maintaining physical health. I honestly couldn't believe how ignorant I was about health awareness. I didn't know there was a difference between HIV and AIDS. I learned that HIV is a virus which destroys the immune system. When the immune system does not work properly for a long period of time, the results will be the development of opportunistic infection(s) which gives the diagnosis of AIDS. I also learned that you can be HIV positive and not have AIDS. However, you cannot have AIDS without being HIV positive.

What does the acronym HIV mean?

H = Human - it only affects humans.

I = Immunodeficiency - the immune system does not work properly.

V = Virus — an organism that must reside inside another cell to reproduce.

What does the acronym AIDS mean?

A = Acquired - a person must get infected; not passed down through genes.

I = Immuno — it affects the body's immune system.

D = Deficiency - the defense system is underperforming.

S = Syndrome - a series of many symptoms, diseases, opportunistic infections (OI's).

Positive Psychology

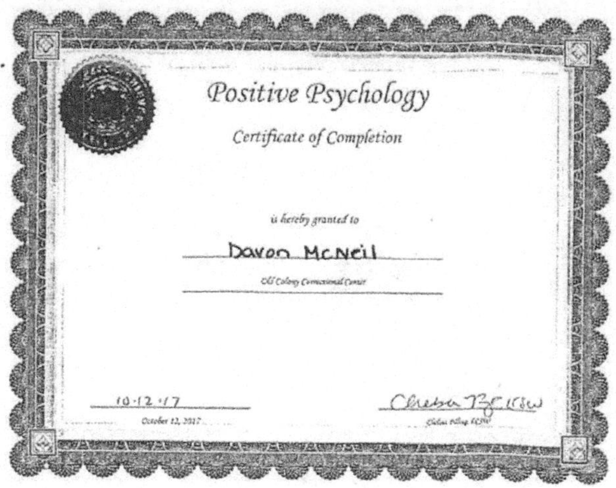

Positive Psychology

Certificate of Completion

is hereby granted to

Davon McNeil

10-12-17

I consider myself to be an overall positive person. However, this state of mind was constructed through hard work and many severe crucibles. I had to literally travel deep within my core self and face many .old internal wounds from childhood. Positive psychology focuses on the positive events and influence in a person's life, including: 1) Positive experiences such as happiness, joy, inspiration, love and 2) positive states and traits like gratitude, residence and compassion. This program is important for those of us who've spent a significant amount of years in prison. Prison is a very hostile and negative environment. It is easy for a person to lose focus by getting sucked into the ominous energy which permeates within the atmosphere of prison. We spent a lot of time in the group discussing topics such as character strengths, optimism, life satisfaction, well-being, self-esteem, self-confidence and elevation.

DAVON MCNEIL

Addiction Psychotherapy

CERTIFICATE OF COMPLETION

Second Time

THIS CIRCLE KEEPER'S CERTIFICATE

IS AWARDED TO

Davon McNeil

THIS 26 DAY OF March, 2019

IN RECOGNITION OF LEADERSHIP IN THE

RESTORATIVE JUSTICE READING GROUP

THIS GROUP INCLUDES RESTORATIVE JUSTICE READINGS, WRITING ASSIGNMENTS AND DISCUSSIONS INTENDED TO DEEPEN PARTICIPANTS' KNOWLEDGE OF RESTORATIVE PRACTICES.

The addiction psychotherapy program served those of us who have acknowledged a history of substance use and addictive behaviors. The intrinsic benefits of this group allowed the participants to draw strength and learn from each other's stories and experiences. This was a 12- week program so we witnessed the growth and recovery of the others in the program while increasing our social connectivity and mutual understanding. We learned effective methods to communicate our needs and emotions while developing skills to recognize and confront the various forms of denial which accompanies addiction. We were able to learn and relearn ways to cope with life's many stressors without the use of illicit substances or addictive behaviors with the hope of positive correction and change.

Emotional Awareness

I really enjoyed and learned a lot about myself by participating in this Emotional Awareness program. This was a psycho-educational group designed to help the men identify their core emotions and what they look like; how they present themselves in a variety of ways; and how they connect to secondary and tertiary (third in order, degree, or rank) feelings. I learned that anger is not a primary emotion; that there are always core emotions which trigger anger. And I also learned about emotional control and regulation. This program was very helpful and informative.

DAVON MCNEIL

Lifer's Psychotherapy

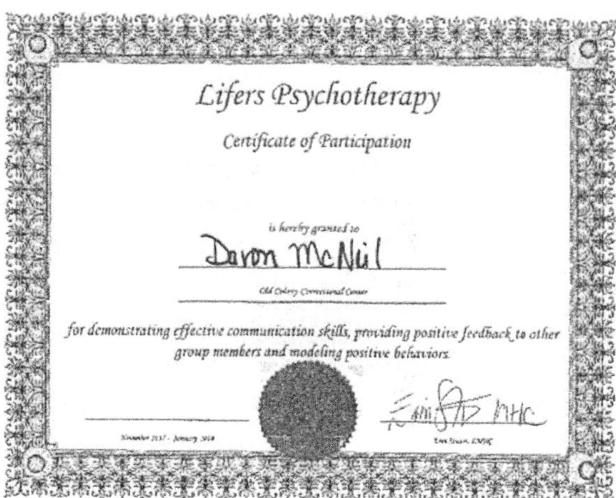

Lifers Psychotherapy

Certificate of Participation

is hereby granted to

Davon McNeil

for demonstrating effective communication skills, providing positive feedback to other group members and modeling positive behaviors.

This was a process-oriented group designed to address concerns specific to individuals serving life sentences through facilitated discussions. I was able to gain a great deal of insight from the men who participated in this program as the majority of them are serving natural life sentences. I'm serving a second-degree life sentence which allows me the opportunity of going before a parole board after serving 15 years of my life in prison. Therefore, the men who are serving natural life made sure I understood how fortunate I was to have another chance at living my life in the outside world. We have all suffered much loss during our time in prison so it was very hard for me to hear these men speak about possibly dying in prison. I will never fully grasp what serving a natural life sentence does to a man's psyche, but I assure you I will never forget what was shared!

Character Exploration

A really good friend of mine recommended that I sign up for this program. My good friend has been incarcerated for 43 years. He and I have engaged in some very intense discussions about character flaws and how they affect our everyday lives and relationships. We had a great group of men who participated in this program. I learned about the concept of Habit-Self and Inner-Self. The habit-self is the part of you that is ruled by habits. It is the voice in your head that automatically says things about what you like or dislike or what you want to do. The habit-self does not think. It just reacts to feelings and memory. Too often the habit-self reacts with "toughness" or with a "get out of my face" attitude. The inner self is the part of you that is responsible, thoughtful and reasonable. We all have an inner-self. It does not get triggered into aggression or defensiveness like the habit-self. I learned to strengthen my inner-self because that is the part of me that can learn and retrain my habit-self in a positive direction. The inner-self, once recognized, can help build a strong character.

Healing from the Past

Healing from the Past

Certificate of Completion

is hereby granted to

Devon McNeil

Old Colony Correctional Center

for completion of the Healing from the Past Group

In this program, we formed a large group and discussed how stressful past experiences can continue to impact our lives and our relationships. We talked about developing and practicing coping skills to manage distress related to PTSD (post-traumatic stress disorder), substance abuse and chronic stress. I learned to take some time every day to be silent and turn inward to start the process of healing from my past. Healing from my past involves being sensitive and concerned for others as well as looking at life and people more positively.

Note: Remembering the problems, pain and identity of the past helps you to stay committed to the struggle of the present and goals of the future. This reminder also underscores the importance of personal humility and the danger of overconfidence. Change and progress can be misleading. Change is a continuing process. Remembering this helps counter the sense of entitlement and narcissism that are characteristic of criminal behavior. It also strengthens identification with and compassion for others in the struggle as well as for us.

Anger Management

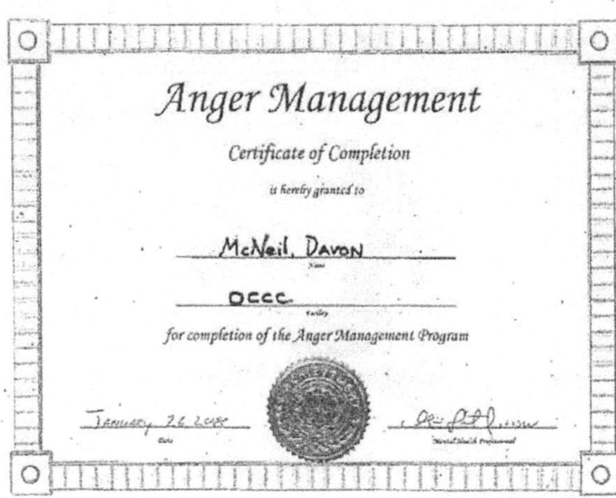

Anger Management

Certificate of Completion

is hereby granted to

McNeil, Davon

OCCC

for completion of the Anger Management Program

During my incarceration. I've always taken advantage of all the available anger management programs/groups. In this particular program, I learned constructive coping skills and how to turn anger into passion in the pursuit of better ideals and goals such as positive growth, academic excellence and social advancement as well as how to verbally express my anger versus acting out the emotion. I feel as though all incarcerated men should participate in this program, especially those who have been convicted of violent offenses. If we're truly serious about changing our lives, we must understand the danger of repressed anger.

Life After Release

This program was very informative because we had a large group of guys who shared a desire to get out of prison and stay out. Unfortunately, most of us had served jail or prison time in the past so we were honestly striving to learn new and positive ways to adjust in society after spending decades of our lives in prison. Each of us received information and training in skills (e.g. cognitive, emotional, behavioral, self-esteem and self-regulation) to increase our success in living a successful, healthy and crime-free life outside of prison. We all agreed that the youths in our communities need us.

Perfect Attendance (Life After Release)

Certificate of Completion

Life After Release

Perfect Attendance

is hereby granted to

Davon McNeil

Old Colony Correctional Center

7/24/18

Date

I know for a fact that my mother and grandmother would be so proud of me for getting perfect attendance in these programs. If only they could see the young man I've grown up to be. I will spend the rest of my life as a change agent and youth advocate.

Perfect Attendance (Positive Psychology)

I was selected to return to the Restorative Justice program as a circle keeper. As a circle keeper it was my responsibility to help the new members of the circle feel comfortable about talking in the group. Also, I explained exactly what the program was about and my past experiences while participating in the program for the very first time. The circle brings together all justice participants, including members of the broader community, to speak about crime and its effects. While seated in a circle, each participant talks about why they're participating. The circle members then create a plan for the offending members to make amends to the victim and community as well as address the causes of the crime. I really enjoyed helping other men open up about their past. We're all on the healing path.

Certificate of Perfect Attendance (Character Exploration Group)

Certificate of Perfect Attendance

is hereby granted to

Davon McNeil

Old Colony Correctional Center

for completion of the Character Exploration Group

November 06, 2018

Diana O'Toole MS

I didn't finish school and I regret it! So I decided to complete every single program in which I participated, even if I didn't enjoy being there. I was taught to take the best parts for myself and leave (what I considered) the poor parts alone.

The 70 x 7 Program
Forgiveness with an Emphasis on Restorative Justice

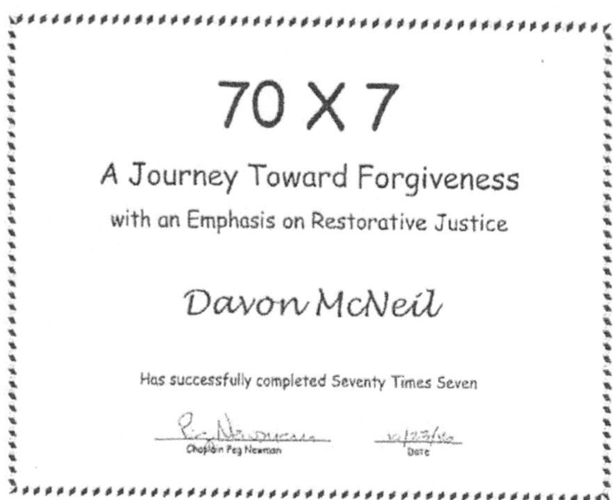

When Peter asked Jesus, "How many times must I forgive., .as many as seven times?" And Jesus replied, "No, seventy times seven." This 12-week program is not religious but is helpful to anyone who struggles to forgive others, or to ask for forgiveness, or to forgive themselves. Through class exercises, DVD's, group discussions and weekly homework assignments, participants come to understand the social, emotional, physical and spiritual price they pay when they are unable to forgive. Emphasis is placed on understanding and working through the seven stages that a person may go through when trying to forgive.

For a person in prison, forgiving himself can be the most difficult kind of forgiveness to achieve. Restorative justice offers an approach that can lead to healing for the person in prison and can also heal what is broken within a family, in the community, or in another setting. Participants explore the effects of their crime on the victim(s); those directly and indirectly affected. However, owning and taking responsibility for their choices and behaviors is only the first step. Participants will also explore what others have done in this area of restoration; what the person can do toward restorative justice while they're in prison; and, if they will be returning to their community, what things they can do when they get home. These types of programs are my absolute favorites.

Peer Support Group

This group was about prisoners encouraging each other to use their time in prison wisely. We were instructed to view prison as a community. Therefore, community members are not only responsible for themselves but also for the well-being of their fellow peers and community. Thus, personal dignity is respected and humiliation is not permitted The program required peers to responsibly address proscribed behaviors and attitudes among one another. We discussed how responsible concern and peer feedback is an essential component of the social-learning environment. Over the years, I learned a lot horn participating in these types of structured programs.

Advanced Anger Management

Advanced Anger Management

Certificate of Completion

is hereby granted to

Davon McNeil

OCCC

for completion of the Advanced Anger Management Program

This was a very intense program and some of the men who started the program with me didn't finish with me. We really went deep into our childhoods to uncover some of the unresolved issues that may have contributed to our deep-rooted anger. Please understand that trauma is a very real thing. I witnessed men 50 and 60 years old speak for the first time about being physically, mentally and sexually abused when they were young children. Some of these men had been holding onto these traumas for decades and cried tears of relief after finally releasing all of the pent up anger they had been carrying. This group was very humbling for me and showed me the power of speaking freely about your past in order to heal from anger.

Who Am I?

I exist in the now-a-day as a conscious (awake, aware, enlightened) thinking black man who has made the responsible choice to take my life into my own hands. First, I had to sit quietly with myself and travel within the inner realms of my mind to silence the negative voice which for many years dictated my ways and actions, thus leading me down many dark, lonely, painful, deceptive and crooked paths.

The greatest battle I've ever had to fight was with myself. I came to the Divine Realization that my entire world was first structured within the chamber of Jerusalem (my mind). My thoughts were, and still are the foundation of my life, past and present.

I AM GREAT! I am able to achieve any goal that I'm laser-focused on. Being firmly rooted within a state of positive thinking allows me to detect static energy (negative vibes) which helps me to navigate around a potential stumbling block.

I'm an empathetic, emotional, caring, compassionate and sensitive being. Suffering has brought true meaning to my life; has forced me to get in touch with a side of myself that I never knew existed (my conscience). In Webster's New World Dictionary, conscience is defined as: a sense of right and wrong; feelings which keep an individual from doing bad things; making someone feel guilty.

I am equality. Equality is a rule I strive to manifest through my ways and actions. Equality is being equal in all things. Equality is being able to secure a degree of balance in one's life.

As I end this scribe, I want to mention that I'm a young man striving to learn how to be a better man each and every day in each and every way. The power of God dwells within me!

From the mind of,
Davon McNeil

Project Youth

By MCI Shirley staff

Project Youth is an interactive awareness program that attempts to show how poor decision making can turn into the stark reality of prison life. Project Youth has hosted high school and college psychology classes, peer pressure advisors, athletic teams, at-risk students and criminal justice programs.

Project Youth was started at Norfolk State Prison in 1964 and was expanded to MCI Shirley Medium in 1993. It is an opportunity for students to have a first-hand account of what life is like in prison. Correctional Officers escort the students to the visiting room of the medium security facility and then they have the opportunity to hear from a selected number of screened inmates in a secure setting. Department staff remain in the visiting room with the students at all times.

Me, sitting behind the speaker during one of our project youth sessions.

Project Youth is a two hour program that includes inmate speakers as well as an engaging question and answer session. Project Youth is not a "Scared Straight" program and no intimidation of the students is allowed. All inmate speakers are required to deliver an honest account of their lives. They discuss the consequences of drug and alcohol involvement, peer pressure, and the behavioral patterns that led to their eventual incarceration.

The highlight of the Project Youth presentation is the question and answer session in which students can ask or write questions that are directed to the inmate panel. All topics are open for discussion. A typical inmate panel would consist of ten inmates ages 20 to 50 who are serving different types of sentences for robbery, assault, murder, weapons charges and white collar crime. No sex offenders are allowed in this program.

The inmates have worked with Recreational Officer II Martin Murphy to put together a pamphlet that is given to all the students who attend. The pamphlet includes ideas that the inmates want the students to take away from the program. A quote from the brochure is: "One of the things we like to stress at Project Youth, is that you will face many difficulties in life but you do not have to face them alone. Your parents and teachers are there for you even if you think they're not. They will take the shirt off their back for you. Talk to them. You will be quite surprised at just how helpful they can be; no matter what it is."

Students listen intently and ultimately realize that the choice that these various inmates made that led them into the state prison system is something that could very well happen to them. Each of the inmate's stories is relatable to many teenagers' lives. They emphasize how drunk driving after a party could result in another's death. Students begin to realize how experimenting with drugs could easily turn into an addiction, and how hanging around with the wrong group of people can incite bad behavior or create a situation of guilt by association.

Project Youth at MCI Shirley medium security facility, hosts an average of two schools a week throughout the school year. The institution has several partnerships with different high schools and colleges throughout the North Central section of Massachusetts. The program has been met with great success and with that success, Project Youth is securing its longevity here at MCI Shirley.

Project Youth
By MCI Shirley staff

Project Youth is an interactive awareness program that attempts to show how poor decision making can turn into the stark reality of prison life. Project Youth has hosted high school and college psychology classes, peer pressure advisors, athletic teams, at-risk students and criminal justice programs.

Project Youth was started at Norfolk State Prison in 1964 and was expanded to MCI Shirley Medium in 1993. It is an opportunity for students to have a first-hand account of what life is like in prison. Correctional Officers escort the students to the visiting room of the medium security facility and then they have the opportunity to hear from a selected number of screened inmates in a secure setting. Department staff remain in the visiting room with the students at all times.

Project Youth is a two hour program that includes inmate speakers as well as an engaging question and answer session. Project Youth is not a "Scared Straight" program and no intimidation of the students is allowed. All inmate speakers are required to deliver an honest account of their lives. They discuss the consequences of drug and alcohol involvement, peer pressure, and the behavioral patterns that led to their eventual incarceration.

The highlight of the Project Youth presentation is the question and answer session in which students can ask or write questions that are directed to the inmate panel. All topics are open for discussion. A typical inmate panel would consist of ten inmates ages 20 to 50 who are serving different types of sentences for robbery, assault, murder, weapons charges and white collar crime. No sex offenders are allowed in this program.

The inmates have worked with Recreational Officer II Martin Murphy to put together a pamphlet that is given to all the students who attend. The pamphlet includes ideas that the inmates want the students to take away from the program. A quote from the brochure is: "One of the things we like to stress at Project Youth, is that you will face many difficulties in life but you do not have to face them alone. Your parents and teachers are there for you even if you think they're not. They will take the shirt off their back for you. Talk to them. You will be quite surprised at just how helpful they can be; no matter what it is."

Students listen intently and ultimately realize that the choice that these various inmates made that led them into the state prison system is something that could very well happen to them. Each of the inmate's stories is relatable to many teenagers' lives. They emphasize how drunk driving after a party could result in another's death. Students begin to realize how experimenting with drugs could easily turn into an addiction, and how hanging around with the wrong group of people can incite bad behavior or create a situation of guilt by association.

Project Youth at MCI Shirley medium security facility, hosts an average of two schools a week throughout the school year. The institution has several partnerships with different high schools and colleges throughout the North Central section of Massachusetts. The program has been met with great success and with that success, Project Youth is securing its longevity here at MCI Shirley.

December 2, 2013

Dear Davon,

Thank you for writing me and making me aware of Project Youth. I would be interested in having our teens hear from men like you so I have forwarded your letter and brochures to our church program chair to discuss with our youth ministry.

Please remember that God is always with you and stay in prayer.

God bless you,

Rev. Robert Washington

Rev. Robert A. Washington

New Faith Missionary Baptist Church

Feb. 6th, 2014

Dear Officer Murphy, Evans, Davon, John, Shawn, Ray, and Sam--

Thank you very much for spending time with us on Tuesday morning when we attended your wonderful Project Youth Program! Your stories were very powerful! You have clearly learned from your own mistakes in life and have become much better men for it! We appreciate your being willing and courageous enough to share your stories with us and for encouraging us to make healthy choices which will help us in the present and the future. We are very grateful to you and wish you the very best in your own future as well.

With much gratitude from all of us at Ayer Shirley Middle School!!!

Thank you for all that you do for the youth. Sincerely, [illegible]

It was an excellent presentation Gentlemen! Thank you for All you are doing to help kids! -Sharon Webb School Counselor

PROJECT YOUTH QUESTIONNAIRE

Date Attended: 1/9/13

Dear Visiting Youth,

We would appreciate it if you would share your opinions and ideas with us by filling out this Questionnaire. This will be used to assist us in evaluating and improving our presentations. Please fill this out in as much detail as possible and return it to your teacher. Thank you!

Grade: 11 School/Facility CHS (chelmsford high school) Male ☐ Female ☑

1. Which speaker did you find most interesting & why?

Devon because his story was the most interesting. You could tell that he had been through alot and he kept making mistakes but he's gotten wiser and he's much smarter. I also liked how he answered questions.

2. Which topic did you find most interesting & why?

Not really a topic but I liked how they all thought what they did was stupid now that they were caught. It's interesting how one situation where you don't think completely - you get caught

3. Do you have any suggestions on how to improve this program?

maybe take kids to empty cells. like a tour of the jail.

4. Are there any topics that you feel were not adequately covered?

The living conditions of jail.

5. What impressed you the most about the Project Youth Program?

How well organized it is and how they chose a group of people with different stories + backgrounds

PLEASE USE THE OTHER SIDE IF NECESSARY

DAVON MCNEIL

Project Youth Questionnaire

Date Attended: 1/15/13

Dear Visiting Youth,

We would appreciate it if you would share your opinions and ideas with us by filling out this questionnaire. This will be used to assist us in evaluating and improving our presentations. Please fill this out in as much detail as possible and return it to your teacher. Thank you!

Grade: 11 School/Facility: Chelmsford High School Male ☐ Female ☑

1. Which speaker did you find most interesting & why?

Davon was the most interesting speaker because of his story he told. Davon had an amazing way with words which helped him get his message across more clearly. Davon was also the most relatable, to me anyway, making his situation easier to understand.

2. Which topic did you find most interesting and why?

The topic I found most interesting was when the men talked about how they all wanted succes in life but that in order to achieve that you need to know how far you are willing to go.

3. Do you have any suggestions on how to improve this program?

The way the program was run was well organized and memorable. I would not suggest any changes except that I would have liked to hear more from some of the men that did not speak as much as others.

4. Are there any topics that you feel were not adequately covered?

I think each topic was covered adequetely and in great detail.

5. What impressed you the most about the Project Youth Program?

What impressed me the most was that the men who participated on the panel were not scary or mean, they were kind fathers, and brothers just like everyone else, they were not perfect they were just human. Going into prison was a new experience and I expected hardened criminals and what I saw instead ... that there are good people in the

~~Please use the other side if necessary.~~

Project Youth Questionnaire

Date Attended: Jan 15 13

Dear Visiting Youth,

We would appreciate it if you would share your opinions and ideas with us by filling out this questionnaire. This will be used to assist us in evaluating and improving our presentations. Please fill this out in as much detail as possible and return it to your teacher. Thank you!

Grade: 11 School/Facility: Chelmsford High Male ☐ Female ☑

1. Which speaker did you find most interesting & why?

Devyn because of his love for his children and seeing him being so positive. Also because he shot the person so quickly and didn't think before makes me sad.

2. Which topic did you find most interesting and why?

the topic I found most interesting was when they said catch your friend from slipping - if they're going down the wrong path, tell them - and I have done that.

3. Do you have any suggestions on how to improve this program?

Maybe if the inmates could ask us questions & have us kids be more honest & at some point make the chaperon leave because we feel nervous. (if we could see their cells)

4. Are there any topics that you feel were not adequately covered?

there stories were kind of confusing, the way they said it

5. What impressed you the most about the Project Youth Program?

How nice & amazing the inmates are. they're normal people who have just made mistakes

Please use the other side if necessary.

DAVON MCNEIL

Project Youth Questionnaire

Date Attended: 1/15/13

Dear Visiting Youth,

We would appreciate it if you would share your opinions and ideas with us by filling out this questionnaire. This will be used to assist us in evaluating and improving our presentations. Please fill this out in as much detail as possible and return it to your teacher. Thank you!

Grade: 11 School/Facility: Chelmsford High Male ☐ Female ☒

1. Which speaker did you find most interesting & why?

I found them all interesting but Davon was the best. He had a lot of detail in his story and showed a lot of emotion allowing us to see how he felt.

2. Which topic did you find most interesting and why?

The topic I found interesting was when they told us why they were in jail and for how long.

3. Do you have any suggestions on how to improve this program?

No, it was really good.

4. Are there any topics that you feel were not adequately covered?

Nope.

5. What impressed you the most about the Project Youth Program?

The way they were able to connect w/ the audience and inspire us really impressed me.

Please use the other side if necessary.

Project Youth Questionnaire

Date Attended: 1/15/13

Dear Visiting Youth,

We would appreciate it if you would share your opinions and ideas with us by filling out this questionnaire. This will be used to assist us in evaluating and improving our presentations. Please fill this out in as much detail as possible and return it to your teacher. Thank you!

Grade: 11 School/Facility: Chelmsford High Male ☐ Female ☒

1. Which speaker did you find most interesting & why?

I found them all interesting but Davon was the best. He had a lot of detail in his story and showed a lot of emotion allowing us to see how he felt.

2. Which topic did you find most interesting and why?

The topic I found interesting was when they told us why they were in jail and for how long.

3. Do you have any suggestions on how to improve this program?

No, it was really good.

4. Are there any topics that you feel were not adequately covered?

Nope.

5. What impressed you the most about the Project Youth Program?

The way they were able to connect w/ the audience and inspire us really impressed me.

Please use the other side if necessary.

Project Youth Questionnaire

Date Attended: January 15th, 2013

Dear Visiting Youth,

We would appreciate it if you would share your opinions and ideas with us by filling out this questionnaire. This will be used to assist us in evaluating and improving our presentations. Please fill this out in as much detail as possible and return it to your teacher.. Thank you!

Grade: 12 School/Facility: Chelmsford High Male ☐ Female ☑

1. Which speaker did you find most interesting & why?

Davon. He had a connection with girls our age because of his daughters. He had a lot of good advice to give us being a young parent.

2. Which topic did you find most interesting and why?

I thought their background and how they were raised was the most interesting. Many of them came from a single home and were involved with drugs.

3. Do you have any suggestions on how to improve this program?

Having two breaks would be a good idea so students sitting in the same seat for hours straight. Split us into smaller groups.

4. Are there any topics that you feel were not adequately covered?

We read about their daily routines but I feel the inmates should have expressed their views on the routine / what they wish the had time for.

5. What impressed you the most about the Project Youth Program?

The inmates were respectful and didn't hesitate to answer any of our questions.

Please use the other side if necessary.

Project Youth Questionnaire

Date Attended: 10/29/13

Dear Visiting Youth,

We would appreciate it if you would share your opinions and ideas with us by filling out this questionnaire. This will be used to assist us in evaluating and improving our presentations. Please fill this out in as much detail as possible and return it to your teacher. Thank you!

Grade: Senior School/Facility: Merrimack College Male ☐ Female ☑

1. Which speaker did you find most interesting & why?

Davon. how he grew up in a home where crime was prominent. we got the full background story: as to how he ended up in prison

2. Which topic did you find most interesting and why?

I liked the debate we had about Amanda Cox's case about whether it was fair or unfair It was interesting to get their views on current events occuring in the world

3. Do you have any suggestions on how to improve this program?

hearing more about others' stories of how they ended up in prison, need more of a background

4. Are there any topics that you feel were not adequately covered?

What their thought's and plans are for the future if/when they get out of prison more about life in prison, ie. relationship w/ guards, scheduling, ect.

5. What impressed you the most about the Project Youth Program?

how respectful the speakers were, how prepared the speakers were, how eager they were to inform us about visiting process/life

Please use the other side if necessary.

DAVON MCNEIL

PROJECT YOUTH QUESTIONNAIRE

Date Attended: 11/12/13

Dear Visiting Youth,

We would appreciate it if you would share your opinions and ideas with us by filling out this Questionnaire. This will be used to assist us in evaluating and improving our presentations. Please fill this out in as much detail as possible and return it to your teacher. Thank you!

Grade: 12 School/Facility Acton - Boxborough Male [ ] Female [X]

1. Which speaker did you find most interesting & why?

I enjoyed Devon's talk because he was the only one able to talk about his story in detail. They were all really interesting though because they were able to talk about their stories ~~[illegible]~~ with confidence

2. Which topic did you find most interesting & why?

Talking about the drug life in prison and all the things that go on in it surprised me. I never would have thought about any of the things that happened to them in prison

3. Do you have any suggestions on how to improve this program?

I think each speaker should be able to tell their story in detail. For time, make each one shorter but still in depth.

4. Are there any topics that you feel were not adequately covered?

No

5. What impressed you the most about the Project Youth Program?

I learned so many new things from this program but what truly impressed me the most was the attitude and courage these speakers have. They all seem like genuienly good people and it was an honor to hear about their life and rough times.

PLEASE USE THE OTHER SIDE IF NECESSARY

PROJECT YOUTH QUESTIONNAIRE

Date Attended: 11/12/13

Dear Visiting Youth,

We would appreciate it if you would share your opinions and ideas with us by filling out this Questionnaire. This will be used to assist us in evaluating and improving our presentations. Please fill this out in as much detail as possible and return it to your teacher. Thank you!

Grade: 12 School/Facility ABRHS Male ☑ Female ☐

1. Which speaker did you find most interesting & why?
   Davon, He had a very interesting story and got emotional.

2. Which topic did you find most interesting & why?
   Prison cliques, and lifestyle

3. Do you have any suggestions on how to improve this program?
   NO.

4. Are there any topics that you feel were not adequately covered?
   no.

5. What impressed you the most about the Project Youth Program?
   How they all seemed like good guys.

PLEASE USE THE OTHER SIDE IF NECESSARY

DAVON MCNEIL

PROJECT YOUTH QUESTIONNAIRE

Date Attended: 11/17

Dear Visiting Youth,

We would appreciate it if you would share your opinions and ideas with us by filling out this Questionnaire. This will be used to assist us in evaluating and improving our presentations. Please fill this out in as much detail as possible and return it to your teacher. Thank you!

Grade: 12 School/Facility Acton Boxboro Regional HS Male ☐ Female ☑

1. Which speaker did you find most interesting & why?

Devon because I thought his message was the most meaningful

2. Which topic did you find most interesting & why?

I liked their example of the party and the saying "kid choices have kid consequences, adult choices have adult consequences".

3. Do you have any suggestions on how to improve this program?

It would be interesting to hear everyone's story of how they ended up there in more depth.

4. Are there any topics that you feel were not adequately covered?

It would be nice to hear about the day to day life.

5. What impressed you the most about the Project Youth Program?

How much you can relate to them even with such different backgrounds.

PLEASE USE THE OTHER SIDE IF NECESSARY

PROJECT YOUTH QUESTIONNAIRE

Date Attended: 11/13

Dear Visiting Youth,

We would appreciate it if you would share your opinions and ideas with us by filling out this Questionnaire. This will be used to assist us in evaluating and improving our presentations. Please fill this out in as much detail as possible and return it to your teacher. Thank you!

Grade: 12 School/Facility ABRHS Male ☐ Female ☒

1. Which speaker did you find most interesting & why?
David. I really liked hearing his whole story. I liked that he is very honest and got quite emotional.

2. Which topic did you find most interesting & why?
Admitting their mistakes they have done and trying to prevent us from doing the same ones.

3. Do you have any suggestions on how to improve this program?
Be less manipulative if they were at all. I didnt really notice and thought that they were nice.

4. Are there any topics that you feel were not adequately covered?
not really

5. What impressed you the most about the Project Youth Program?
How we were able to ask any questions we wanted

PLEASE USE THE OTHER SIDE IF NECESSARY

DAVON MCNEIL

PROJECT YOUTH QUESTIONNAIRE

Date Attended: 12/10

Dear Visiting Youth,

We would appreciate it if you would share your opinions and ideas with us by filling out this Questionnaire. This will be used to assist us in evaluating and improving our presentations. Please fill this out in as much detail as possible and return it to your teacher. Thank you!

Grade: 12 School/Facility Dracut High School Male ☐ Female ☑

1. Which speaker did you find most interesting & why?
Devon was the most interesting because he got straight to the point, and he seemed remorseful for what happened

2. Which topic did you find most interesting & why?
I think their stories because it could happen to anyone.

3. Do you have any suggestions on how to improve this program?
I think they should have all the prisoners tell their story.

4. Are there any topics that you feel were not adequately covered?
I think we should've talked more about how they felt

5. What impressed you the most about the Project Youth Program?
The attitude of the prisoners

PLEASE USE THE OTHER SIDE IF NECESSARY

PROJECT YOUTH QUESTIONNAIRE

Date Attended: 12/10

Dear Visiting Youth,

We would appreciate it if you would share your opinions and ideas with us by filling out this Questionnaire. This will be used to assist us in evaluating and improving our presentations. Please fill this out in as much detail as possible and return it to your teacher. Thank you!

Grade: 11 School/Facility [illegible] High Male ☐ Female ☑

1. Which speaker did you find most interesting & why?

I found Davon more interesting because he told his story a lot better and really kept you interested.

2. Which topic did you find most interesting & why?

I liked the questions because I felt you got to get a little more detail. Plus you could get to know more about the others who didn't get to fully share their story.

3. Do you have any suggestions on how to improve this program?

Nope

4. Are there any topics that you feel were not adequately covered?

I wanted to know more about life in prison and how different it is compared to what we know.

5. What impressed you the most about the Project Youth Program?

The fact that you got to really understand their stories and how I went in with a totally different outlook then I came out with.

PLEASE USE THE OTHER SIDE IF NECESSARY

Project Youth Questionnaire

Date Attended: Feb. 4th

Dear Visiting Youth,

We would appreciate it if you would share your opinions and ideas with us by filling out this questionnaire. This will be used to assist us in evaluating and improving our presentations. Please fill this out in as much detail as possible and return it to your teacher. Thank you!

Grade: 8 School/Facility: Ayer Shirley Male ☐ Female ☒

1. Which speaker did you find most interesting & why?

The speaker I found most interesting was Davon, I liked his story and the way he talked about his experiences

2. Which topic did you find most interesting and why?

I found it interesting when they talked about their families

3. Do you have any suggestions on how to improve this program?

no, I think it was very good.

4. Are there any topics that you feel were not adequately covered?

I thought that I wanted to know more about the day in the life of a prisoner

5. What impressed you the most about the Project Youth Program?

It suprised me about the way the prisoners were open, and very hearted and open about there stories.

Please use the other side if necessary.

Project Youth Questionnaire

Date Attended: Feb 4th, 2014

Dear Visiting Youth,

We would appreciate it if you would share your opinions and ideas with us by filling out this questionnaire. This will be used to assist us in evaluating and improving our presentations. Please fill this out in as much detail as possible and return it to your teacher.. Thank you!

Grade: Chaperone School/Facility: Ayer Shirley Middle School Male ☐ Female ☒

1. Which speaker did you find most interesting & why?

Davon - A good story teller & kept it interesting. Also emphasized his own mistakes & really gave a good warning to our girls.

2. Which topic did you find most interesting and why?

3. Do you have any suggestions on how to improve this program?

I Appreciated John's message but thought he went on speaking for too long - the kids were getting restless.

4. Are there any topics that you feel were not adequately covered?

5. What impressed you the most about the Project Youth Program?

Evans did a great job as the MC / I really liked & Appreciated how All of the men emphasized how important it is to make good choices & how one big mistake can result in long-term consequences

Please use the other side if necessary.

THE
LIONHEART
FOUNDATION

Davon Mcneil
P.O. Box 1218
Shirley, Medium
Shirley, MA 01464

Dear Davon,

Just a quick note to say again that I'm glad I could help.

I am grateful that Houses of Healing has played a part in opening the door to your "inner child". It sounds like you are doing some wonderful healing work. It takes real openness and courage to do this work in a deep way. Great for you, Davon, that you are willing to do this. I also think it is a long-term commitment. Little Davon needs to know that you are going to be there for him.

I imagine it is quite challenging to go through the holiday season behind the walls, but at the same time, I hope you increasingly feel connected to the amazing person within.

I am enclosing a few things that you might enjoy and find useful.

Blessings and Best wishes – May 2014 be a great year for you.

Robin

Robin

PO Box ~~194 Back Bay~~ 170115 · Boston, MA 02117 · Tel. 781-444-6667 · Fax 781-444-6855 · www.lionheart.org

209H6504

Birthing the Male Spirit
Blase Provitola

June 4, 2015

Chairperson Bonner
Massachusetts State Parole Board
12 Mercer Rd.
Natick, Ma. 01760

Re: Parole Board Hearing of Mr. Davon McNeil W- 82395
Dear Chairperson Bonner and Parole Board Members:

This is a letter of recommendation for Mr. Davon McNeil. Mr. McNeil has been a student of the Menswork course at MCI Shirley. My name is Blase W. Provitola and I am the co-founder and facilitator of Menswork at MCI Shirley (Medium). Mensworkinc. is a non-profit organization committed to the rehabilitation of incarcerated men through 10-12 week programs in personal responsibility and self awareness. Additionally graduates have opportunity to participate in our ongoing Menswork Men's Circle. Both of these classes address addiction as well as domestic violence and their underlying issues. Based upon years of volunteer service in the prison community, Menswork teaches that change is possible and that each individual has the ability to choose and rebuild his life. Our emphasis is one of introspection, living sober, and empowering incarcerated men to be productive non violent members of society.

Mr. McNeil is a graduate of our 12 week Menswork course at MCI Shirley. At MCI Shirley he has participated from April 12 – June 21, 2011 and graduated. As a class member, Mr. McNeil has participated and completed all the work necessary to graduate. Additionally Mr. McNeil has co-facilitated with me from Sept. 20 - Dec. 13, 2011 and presented class material. He was a member of our Menswork Men's Circle since April of 2011 - July 2014. In the time that I have known Mr. McNeil he has been positive and participates actively in class to learn more about his self. Mr. McNeil shows up consistently to class and is helpful with other men. He is an active listener and contributes regularly to our Men's Circle. Thanks for permission to write this letter of recommendation.

Sincerely Yours,

Blase W. Provitola
Executive Director

38 Eldridge Rd. Harvard. Ma. 01451

DAVON MCNEIL

The Commonwealth of
Massachusetts
Executive Office of Public Safety and Security
Department of Correction
Bridgewater State Hospital
20 Administration Rd.
Bridgewater, Massachusetts 02324
(508) 279-4500
www.mass.gov/doc

Charles D. Baker
Governor

Karyn Polito
Lieutenant Governor

Daniel Bennett
Secretary

Carol Higgins O'Brien
Commissioner

Katherine A. Chmiel
Thomas E. Dickhaut
Paul L. DiPaolo
Deputy Commissioners

Veronica Madden
Superintendent

June 3, 2015

Devon McNeil #W82395
Bridgewater State Hospital
20 Administration Road
Bridgewater, MA 02021

Dear Mr. McNeil:

I would like to acknowledge the extra efforts that you made over this winter during our historical snowfalls. The nature of this facility requires patients to go outside to the Commons building for meals and program activities, regardless of weather, and for staff to travel among buildings to perform their duties. Your extra efforts in maintaining continuous shifts of snow removal on our walkways allowed operations to continue normally as much as possible even during blizzard conditions.

Staff was able to provide care and treatment to our patients throughout this incredible winter due to your commitment.

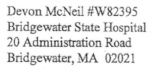

Thank you.

Sincerely,

Veronica Madden
Superintendent

VM/bjm
FRN 15-16

Cc: File

The Commonwealth of Massachusetts
Executive Office of Public Safety and Security
Department of Correction
Bridgewater State Hospital
20 Administration Rd.
Bridgewater, Massachusetts 02324
(508) 279-4500
www.mass.gov/doc

Charles D. Baker
Governor

Karyn Polito
Lieutenant Governor

Daniel Bennett
Secretary

Thomas A. Turco III
Commissioner

Katherine A. Chmiel
Thomas E. Dickhaut
Michael G. Grant
Deputy Commissioners

Daniel Calis
Superintendent

Davon McNeil W82395
Bridgewater State Hospital
20 Administration Rd.
Bridgewater, MA 02321

April 11, 2016

Dear Mr. McNeil,

This letter serves to inform you that I have confirmed your participation in a volunteer facilitated 5-week Re-entry Workshop that was offered at Bridgewater State Hospital every Thursday in the month of March 2016. The topics associated with this workshop are listed below:

3/3- Week 1: Our Identity and the World's Effect on Us.
3/10-Week 2: Communication and Effective Listening
3/17-Week 3: Conflict Resolution
3/24-Week 4: Examining the root cause of Anger
3/31-Week 5: Learning Acceptance

Sincerely,

James Rioux, Director of Classification and Treatment

January 12th 2014

Peace,

GOD Bless. I received your letter and I reread it before answering. You are a developing leader and with that comes a price. There should be no feelings of shame for you did not make the world nor create the conditions that you were raised. You have had doubts, but you must become reassured that you are worthy and not be held hostage to mistakes that you made growing up. Your being incarcerated has allowed you to feel a need for emotional maturity that can only be achieved when you change your thinking, which I believe you have. You will overcome all of this. Malcolm did.

Reading your words about crying is understandable for I "cry" a lot in my heart when I see the eyes of our young People. They eyes have no "sparkle" for hope, but instead are dull like the dead fish that are on display in the fish markets. Your work is important and while you may not think it is, trust and believe it makes People think when I speak about you and your work. I will put more effort in getting you to the next level. I am very happy to know that you are working on getting your IRSBN number from the Library of Congress.

Now that you have written a book, put thoughts on paper for another book. let writing grow in your head and look at things/People as characters for your books. I'm redoing my book of poetry because I think it is good. I mailed you and Salim one of our Black Veterans calendars and I sent one to Norfolk, but it was returned. Did you receive yours? let me know.

Continue to write those that you have written and they will become a base of support for you when it is time for you to see the parole Board. Just keep me posted. I was rushing when I came last, but I need to be invited again and really get down. In the meantime, keep thinking good thoughts and keep a clear mind, we need your mind and thoughts about first being free within ourselves without the baloney. Stay in touch and keep us in prayer.

In the Spirit,

Haywood Fennell, Sr.

Haywood Fennell, Sr.

The Stanley Jones Clean Slate Project, Inc.

"Working for A Better Community"

Board of Fellows:
Heather Parsons. M.S., Loren Earl Roberts, M.S., Milton Jones, Robyn McGrory, Tom Carlson
Stephen Walker, Haywood Fennell,Sr., Founder/President

May 12th 2015

This letter is written based on what I know about Davon and his family who I have been friendly for at least twenty years. For some years Davon lived in Boston and later moved to Brockton into an at risk environment that would cause him to commit a crime that has incarcerated him for some years. I participate in resident's program as an outside guest and it was during a prison program that I came in contact with Davon a few years ago. Davon has a strong testimony and wrote and designed a program to help youth avoid traps that would place them in harm's way for coming to prison. I have presented the document for Davon's program to my Church and to the Massachusetts Association of Minority Law Enforcement Officers (MAMLEO) who both have expressed an interest in the project. Davon has grown and has not allowed himself to not look at his life with the understanding as to what he did was wrong and why he is there. He knows and has spoken about his change. He has recently added Author to his resume in that he has written a book and it is being published. Even though Davon is incarcerated, he has been engaged, learning who he is not realizing that he can and must be a helper and not a hurter with his life. Davon reports that he has been involved throughout his incarceration and completed several offered courses in good standing. He wants to have options when released. The Stanley Jones Clean Slate Project is working with ex-offenders and assisting them with getting the services and care needed through the organizing of a plan. Davon will be faced with many obstacles, but with support and determination to stay focused so that he can change his living, we are willing to help him.

Davon is talented writer, but works to earn a living with a regular job as he learns and realizes that he is a resource and has expressed a desire to work as a volunteer when he can fit our program in our early prevention program by speaking to at risk youth and parents. We are working to develop this program using the talents and voices of folks, male and female who have experienced incarceration. Davon has stated that he wants to participate in any way that he can to help educate and empower the community. It is my hope that this letter of support will facilitate a favorable decision for Mr. Davon McNeil Thank you.

Respectfully submitted,

Haywood Fennell, Sr.

Haywood Fennell, Sr., B .A.

FROM NEGATIVE TO POSITIVE

September 15th 2015

Peace,

There is none greater than GOD and I thank HIM daily and other times for giving us life and the strength and courage to stand. You are in my prayers as I am sure that I am in yours. Accept this communications as a testament to my commitment to our friendship.

I have read your letters and needless to say, it takes a warrior to fight and not whimper. Your freedom when come because you have not allowed a mistake or mistakes to determine who you are. I was recently involved in a campaign seeking to be elected in the primary for the November vote to be the City Councilor from District 7 here in Boston. I placed third. Our People have yet to realize that they cannot expect others to help us, but we must help ourselves. Voying was very light. I had a strong message which moved some in my direction for support and others back into their holes of apathy.

I am getting ready for a family trip to NC and will resume my writings to complete my writing projects. Hope you are writing. It has set me free. I saw your aunt Debbie and she told me about the composition of your team when you went before the Board. You will get that, but plan to have stronger voices on your behalf because you have done some good things and that should not be ignored. Stay at it.

Begin to reach out to other folks in the community and tell them what you have been doing. Promote yourself. Promote your work from where you are. make friends where you can. Trust GOD not Man. Keep the names herein on your list. What is the situation with your book sells if any? Write these People and keep them updated, Rev. Robert A. Washington, New Faith Missionary Baptist Church, 66 Geneva Ave., Dorchester, MA. 02121 and Mr. lLarry Ellison, MAMLEO, Inc., 61 Columbia Rd., Dorchester, MA. 0210. Build your network.

You are doing a lot and I am proud of you. Keep writing and remember to say prayers for us out here and in there. Far too many come out and sit in their own shit and do the same things as before. we need your help. Peace.

Haywood Fennell, Sr.

Haywood Fennell, Sr.

RUTH GREENBERG
--ATTORNEY AT LAW--
505 PARADISE ROAD #166
SWAMPSCOTT, MASSACHUSETTS 01907
(781) 593-5277

April 29, 2015

Board of Parole
Bridgewater State Hospital
20 Administration Road
Bridgewater, MA 02324

Re: Davon McNeil

Dear Members of the Board,

This letter is to recommend Mr. Davon McNeil be paroled.

I have known Mr. McNeil for many years in many contexts. He is an honest person from an honest and supportive large family, whom I have met, and whom I am confident will provide the community support which is so helpful when a person is newly released. Mr. McNeil is not alone in the world. He has family and friends and I am proud to call myself among them.

Mr. McNeil is a person who cares about other people. In the course of the years I have known him, he has always reached out a hand to help a fellow prisoner in need. He has true social skills.

Mr. McNeil is a wonderful writer. The power to express oneself is a good predictor of the power to succeed.

Mr. McNeil is a person of faith and hope. He does not depend on substances for support. He depends on friends and family who help him and whom he helps in return. He is patient and courteous always, and he is able to see the good in the world even when things don't go his way.

Other people have observed these fine qualities and will testify to them. I write to bring one particular matter to the attention of the Board. I am the lawyer who represented Mr. McNeil in his long litigation to protect the right to public trial. I can say that Mr. McNeil did this, not for himself, but for others. His was a test case for a principle of law which had nothing to do with accepting or denying responsibility. It was all about what his family needed, to be with him in court, and what the law needed, clarification of the permissible extent of courtroom closure and the necessity that lawyers know the law. Mr. McNeil took on this litigation knowing it could not possibly be complete in time to secure him any advantage. He did it, at my encouragement, despite the ups and downs, for the sake of the law alone.

In my opinion, and based on my many years of experience, Mr. McNeil presents no future danger to the public whatsoever. If released, he will be a contributor to his family, his community and his church, a good worker, a good writer, and a good friend. I urge the Board to find him a suitable candidate for parole.

Sincerely,

Ruth Greenberg

RG/ls

To: Honourable Parole Board,

Growing up, I ALWAYS looked up to my father. He always made me feel like anything was possible and he could do no wrong in my eyes. Unfortunately, my father made some poor decisions at a very young age that came with consequences that he had to own up to and honestly, I miss my father every single day but I am extremely thankful for these consequences because they saved his life. At such a young age, when my father was incarcerated I did not understand the intricacies of the matter but now that I am older and understand the situation, I look at his incarceration as a mere set back that saved him because if my father continued down that path, that risked the chances of outcomes that are far more dangerous.

Now, the young man that was incarcerated 15 years ago is not the man that I know anymore. The man that I know now is a man that decided that he had choices to make while serving his sentence because there was no way around it. It was either let the situation consume him and stay stagnant in his ways or change his life for the better and not let his past represent his future. This man would enlighten me on all of his positive attributes (internal in his mind) & (externally to his surroundings) to receive the true understandings on becoming a better person. And it is one thing to say you are going to make a change in your life rather than to actually do it and he did it 100 percent. It took him many years of research, studying and retaining knowledge of growth to become this man that is fully aware of his changes and strives for continuous growth upon his freedom. I am ecstatic to say that this man that I speak so highly of is my father.

During my father's incarceration, I decided not to let this situation devalue our relationship because I accepted his poor choices and knew from the very beginning that he would make a change. My father was incarcerated when I was nine years old; I am turning twenty two this year. I speak to my father very often and it is always a conversation full of enlightenment on how I'm doing mentally and what my next goals are, and my eyes flood with tears of joy just knowing in the back of my mind that not only has he became a better person but is instilling these lessons within me to ensure that I become the best version of myself. I'm at a point in my life where I have so many thoughts and ideas of what I should do with my life and what my future withholds and we have such a strong bond that I would automatically go to my dad with any of my ideas and thoughts but it is so difficult with him being away because unfortunately I can't just pick up the phone and call him for advice. At this point in my life I know that is what I nee. After every conversation with my father, I end with such a clear mind and a better understanding on what I need to do to ensure success in my future. My dad puts situations are such perspectives that I would have never thought of and I know that his knowledge is deeply rooted from the transition he made in becoming a better person.

Upon my father's release I can certainly vouch for him when saying he is at peace with his past, accepted it and put it behind him for good. He has tunnel versioned his mind into ideas of positivism and continuing to be a better person. Not only does my father have myself to continue teaching positive attributes but my younger sister as well who is at a point in her life where the real world is starting to set in as a young adult, and it is not only beneficial but crucial that my father be a part of her life during this time.

Sincerely,

Shalese Mcneil

FROM NEGATIVE TO POSITIVE

To whom it may concern:

First would like to introduce myself, my name is Jason McNeil I am the first born grandchild to the McNeil family. I currently live in Dacula, Ga and have four kids and a wife. I'm a graduate of Clark Atlanta University with a BA degree in Art/Graphic Design. After graduating from college I played Pro basketball overseas in China and worked part time at the Boys and Girls club of America in Norcross, Ga for a few years. Once my basketball career was over I joined corporate America. I'm currently the manager of one of Akzo Nobel North America sites. I also started my own company called Fluid Artistry & Design which deals with arts as a whole such as managing local talent in the city, photography, tattoo, mix & mingle, and painting. Devon is my first cousin but more like a little brother to me. Wherever I went he went while growing up as kids. Devon looked up to me like as a positive male role model considering there wasn't any in our family due to the streets, incarceration and drugs. It was very tough growing up in Boston, Ma in the 80 early 90 due to our environment and peer pressure, but for me I wouldn't change it for nothing in the world because it made my drive to be a productive citizens even greater. I moved to Atlanta, Ga in 1989 and graduated from Redan High School before attending college. It may sound strange to say, but I believe being incarcerated has made Devon a stronger and wiser man. Through the years Devon and I have kept in touch I've noticed his growth from being a carefree boy to a conscious man. Everything happens for a reason, and this was a calling for him to use this trying time in his life to do good with mentoring the youth and helping them understand that this is not the life that they want to go through. He's able to share his experience to save the next young man. I always say that kids or young adults can relate more with people who grow up with the same cultural background, rather than some scholar that took a few classes in college about human behaviour. Once Devon is released from prison he will have a mission to stand for. Employment is a must just to stay busy mentally and able to manage a life and help support his two daughters. I'm going to be a part of Devon's mission to guide him in the right direction for success. My first action is taking place as we speak; I'm getting his book "The Streets Lied" published which will create an income for him. Second is helping him join with a non-profit PIM prevention Intervention organization with a few of Boston's community leaders. Devon's mission plan will be a great start and positive motivation for him to transition back into society. I get all tingly inside considering that I know this is going to be a positive and great movement for Devon. Once out he will provide knowledge and understanding to our lost youth. This is basically a short summery on behalf of Devon McNeil to let you the courts know that a lesson has been learned and now it's time for him to help our society because our young adults matter without them we have no future America. Also, I am a strong positive male role model and I plan to help out with Devon's transition on how to be a successful and productive citizen.

Thanks for your time and consideration

Jason McNeil

DAVON MCNEIL

April 15, 2015

Re: Davon Mcneil

To The honorable members of the parole board,

I am writing this letter to support a man that has been a part of my life for more than 22 years. I was 13 years old, he was 15 years old and at the prime of his rage. Davon was my first love.

At the age of 15, 16, 17, years old, Davon was allowed to pretty much do as he pleased. He dropped out of high school in the 9th grade. There were nights he didn't go home. In his mind he was an adult. He actually was. He was to provide for himself by this time. Davon didn't have the guidance that most kids have. And to him this was normal. Everyone who he associated with lived the same way. I was the only person whom to him was "different". I was 13 years old trying to tell him right from wrong. As you can imagine my voice wasn't strong enough.

As a child he had no role model. His father was in and out of jail his entire life. Which also meant, he was in and out of Davon's life, for his entire life. This is the man he is supposed to look to for guidance. So basically he was a child of the streets. Davon was in and out of jail throughout his teen years. Actually, following in his "role models" footsteps. Not that that is an excuse. At some point you know right from wrong. I do believe Davon knew the lifestyle he was living was completely wrong by all means, but I also think that once he was accustomed to living this lifestyle, his vision didn't see another way of living. I do believe that being in prison for the past 14+ years has allowed him to see that there has to be another way, a better way of life.

Along his journey in prison he has lost friends to this lifestyle he used to live. He has lost family members that he will never see again. We have a daughter that was 2 ½ months old when he left. She is now 15 years old. He has missed her entire life. He also has a daughter that is now 22 and he has missed all of her important years as well. He has missed family and loved ones major moments in life. He has witnessed the tragedy of his little brother following in his footsteps. This has not been easy on the man that he is today. He holds guilt for this. He holds guilt for not being in the free world to guide his brothers in a better direction, for not being a good role model, for not being there to watch his daughters grow into beautiful young woman.

Davon is not the child today that he was when he went to prison 15 years ago. If anyone knows that, it's me. I've been on this journey the entire time. Today he is a responsible man that has learned so much. He has taken an abundance of classes that have taught him how to be a better man, father, and citizen. That to me is amazing. Nothing makes me happier or prouder than to see the man that he's become. He is in such a positive space right now. He has removed all of the negative influences from his life and has surrounded himself with great people that are willing to help him when he is released.

What I hope to see from this is Davons freedom. We miss him. I think that he deserves a chance as an adult, as a man, to prove himself not just to us but to himself. I believe he is ready for this chapter in his life. He deserves to be a part of his family's lives. We have had our ups and downs over these 15 years but I love him. He is a great man. I will support him in any way that I can. I have my own home and he will forever have somewhere to live. I have supported him through these 15 years incarcerated and I will continue to support him through the next 15 years. My support will come to him in the form of shelter, food, guidance, and love. I will be there through his every day struggles to help guide him in the right direction. I will do whatever it is that I can for this man, because I love him.

He is a man that is wise beyond his years. Now that he is aware of his greatness and the love and support he has surrounding him, he can only be an amazing man.

Thank you for giving me the opportunity to show my support to Davon Mcneil through this letter.

Davon McNeil
W-82395
20 Administration Road
Bridgewater, MA 02324

Dear Davon,

My name is Elvera Perry and I am the Administrative Manager of Advocacy and Opportunity Youth here at YouthBuild USA. I received your letter in February and you have been on mind ever since. I apologize for the delay in responding to you. I have been busy traveling for work planning events similar to the one you read about in the Boston Banner newspaper. I would like to sincerely thank you for reaching out and for sharing your story. I was highly moved by your biography. You and I are about the same age both from Boston. I unfortunately know too many similar stories which is the reason why I am in this work.

I would also like to thank you for your offer to assist with the growth and development of our movement. I am including our Recommendations to Increase Opportunity and Decrease poverty in America for your review. I would love to receive your feedback. Please let me know if we may we have permission to publish your letter on our website (www.OYUnited.org)? I think your story could inspire so many others. I can tell from your many certificates of achievement that you have indeed changed your life around. So many people go to prison and don't take advantage of the programs available to them. I found it particularly interesting that you had a certificate for the Four Agreements program. I have a printout of the Four Agreements on my desk as a reminder in my day to day life.

I look forward to hearing back from you.
Keep your head up!
Elvera

Spectrum
HEALTH SYSTEMS, INC
Building better lives, one step at a time.

August 5, 2013

Dear Davon McNeil W82395,

You have been selected by the CRA Program Director as a Graduate Support Member who stands out for your positive attitude and exemplary support of this program thus far. I would like to extend the opportunity for you to continue to foster change and growth within the TC as a Graduate Mentor in a leadership role within the GSP Program.

This position may come with high demands and responsibilities and will challenge you as a member of the GSP program, but will give you an opportunity for increased involvement in the leadership of the TC program.

I would like to meet with you in the Voc Ed CRA area on Tuesday, 8/6/13 at 2:30 to discuss this position and give you more information. Please make every effort to attend, as some issues are time sensitive.

Again, congratulations, you have been chosen due to your ongoing commitment to the CRA and GSP program. The staff feel you will make an excellent choice as a leader.

Respectfully,

Jamie Goodgion
CRA Program Director
MCI Shirley

Dear Deron,

Our family is so very grateful for the sincere and heartfelt letters of support you did for Billy to help us try to bring him home during this end-of-life time he has been diagnosed with. In our time of feeling so very helpless, you have made us feel quite hopeful and comforted.

God willing, your efforts will be instrumental in allowing us to personally care for our husband, dad, and grandfather firsthand. And may Billy's success in a compassionate release be the beginning of what is needed throughout the correctional system.

Our sincere and humble thanks to you all.

Donna Barnoski

Ashley Barnoski

Susie Gallagher

Grace Gallagher

Liam

The Barnoski Family

Matt Gallagher

Sammie Gallagher

Joe Gallagher

FROM : FAX NO. : Jul. 13 2015 10:00AM P10

Graduate Support Rating Form

Graduate Support: McNeil, Davon Date: May 2014 Job Assigned Mentor

DIRECTIONS (Staff): Assess the graduate support member in each of the areas below, using the scale below. Any "D" rating indicating a member does not meet an expectation must include reasons in the "Notes" section and requires a follow up meeting and plan of action with the GSP member.

SCALE: M=Meets expectation D=Does not meet expectation

M **Participates in running evening scheduled programming as assigned and related to specific job assignment.**

M **Infraction free, including DOC disciplinary reports, minor disciplinary reports and CRA interventions.**

M **Attends all required meetings, groups and activities scheduled.**

M **Upholds rules/expectations by giving appropriate awareness to fellow community members whenever necessary.**

M **Upholds community values and rules by maintaining appropriate language and appropriate attire at all times.**

M **Maintains a clean and neat living area and performs any unit jobs/duties as assigned.**

M **Communicates respectfully with all staff and program members, and responds appropriately and respectfully when given corrective feedback or awareness.**

NOTES: Inmate McNeil continues to demonstrate a pos. Recovery attitude in the program.

Staff Signature Sara [illegible] Cp Counselor Date 5/23/14

DAVON MCNEIL

Graduate Support Rating Form

Graduate Support: McNeil, Davon Date: June 2014 Job Assigned Mentor

DIRECTIONS (Staff):Assess the graduate support member in each of the areas below, using the scale below. Any "D" rating indicating a member does not meet an expectation must include reasons in the "Notes" section and requires a follow up meeting and plan of action with the GSP member.

SCALE: M=Meets expectation D=Does not meet expectation

M **Participates in running evening scheduled programming as assigned and related to specific job assignment.**

M **Infraction free, including DOC disciplinary reports, minor disciplinary reports and CRA interventions.**

M **Attends all required meetings, groups and activities scheduled.**

M **Upholds rules/expectations by giving appropriate awareness to fellow community members whenever necessary.**

M **Upholds community values and rules by maintaining appropriate language and appropriate attire at all times.**

M **Maintains a clean and neat living area and performs any unit jobs/duties as assigned.**

M **Communicates respectfully with all staff and program members, and responds appropriately and respectfully when given corrective feedback or awareness.**

NOTES: Inmate McNeil continues to comply with all program expectations and demonstrates a pro-recovery attitude in the program.

Staff Signature [signature] GSP Counselor **Date** 6/23/14

FROM NEGATIVE TO POSITIVE

Graduate Support Rating Form

Graduate Support: McNeil, Davon Date: July 2014 Job Assigned: Peer Mentor

DIRECTIONS (Staff): Assess the graduate support member in each of the areas below, using the scale below. Any **"D"** rating indicating a member does not meet an expectation must include reasons in the **"Notes"** section and requires a follow up meeting and plan of action with the GSP member.

SCALE: M=Meets expectation D=Does not meet expectation

M **Participates in running evening scheduled programming as assigned and related to specific job assignment.**

NA **Infraction free, including DOC disciplinary reports, minor disciplinary reports and CRA interventions.**

M **Attends all required meetings, groups and activities scheduled.**

M **Upholds rules/expectations by giving appropriate awareness to fellow community members whenever necessary.**

M **Upholds community values and rules by maintaining appropriate language and appropriate attire at all times.**

M **Maintains a clean and neat living area and performs any unit jobs/duties as assigned.**

M **Communicates respectfully with all staff and program members, and responds appropriately and respectfully when given corrective feedback or awareness.**

NOTES: Inmate was removed from the program unit on 7/15/14.
Inmate was compliant to the expectations prior to him being removed from the program

Staff Signature [illegible] GSP Counselor **Date** 7/25/14

Spectrum Health Systems, Inc.
Graduate Support Program
Discharge Summary

Name: McNeil, Davon No. W82395

DOA: 10/23/12 Site Admitted: MCI-Shirley

DOD: 8/25/14

REASON FOR DISCHARGE FROM TREATMENT: (Check all that apply)

Completion ____ Voluntary Withdrawal ____ Alcohol/Drug Use ____ GCD ____

Disciplinary ____ Medical/MH ____ Non-Compliance ____ Parole ____

Classification: ✓ Other: ____________

Discharge Plan:

Inmate McNeil was compliant throughout this course of treatment. Inmate was discharged from the Graduate Support Program due to being transferred to another institution, as of this writing this file is now closed.

Closed Record
Staff Signature [signature] GSP Counselor Date 8/26/14

McNeil, Devon W 87395 A3 45B

OLD COLONY CORRECTIONAL CENTER

Lib

INMATE WORK ASSIGNMENT

JOB DESCRIPTION

1. **LOCATION OF POSITION:** RECOVERY UNIT

2. **JOB TITLE:** Special Needs Assistant (Companion Program)

3. **HOURS:** To be agreed upon during weekly supervision group.

4. **PAY GRADE:** ~~None.~~ $2.00 day 6 days Eligible for 5 days EGT per month in program/work.

5. **NO. OF DAYS:** Schedule is arranged individually between companion and Unit Director.

6. **NO. OF POSITIONS:** 15 (Max.)

7. **DESCRIPTION OF DUTIES:**

   a. **Daily Tasks**

   - Provide support and encouragement regarding personal hygiene.
   - Encourage involvement of patients in recreation activities.
   - Encourage involvement of patients in programs.
   - Submit daily flow sheet describing that day's activity.

   b. **Weekly Tasks**

   - Meet with companion twice weekly.

   c. **Periodic/As Needed Tasks**

   - Complete initial evaluation.
   - Complete three-month evaluation.
   - Complete one-year evaluation.

8. **SKILLS REQUIRED:**

   a. Relationship skills/desire to help others.
   b. Patience/problem solving skills.
   c. Understanding of mental illness.

9. **SUPERVISION REQUIRED:**

   a. Attend weekly one-hour supervision group facilitated by staff.
   b. Companion's treatment team to review daily flow sheets submitted.

10. **TITLE OF SUPERVISOR:** Deputy Superintendent of Patient Services.

11. **TRAINING REQUIRED:**

   a. Attend 16 hours of specific training prior to assignment as a companion.
   b. Attend on-going weekly training throughout program.

Devon McNeil

INMATE WORKER

ASSIGNMENT OFFICER

4-20-17

DATE

PART THREE

New Program Proposals

by Davon McNeil

Self-Improvement Group/Civilization Class
Program Proposal
November 19, 2014

Cadre, Davon McNeil
Patient, Daryl Golston

8
CHAPTER EIGHT

SELF-IMPROVEMENT GROUP/CIVILIZATION CLASS

Introduction

The Self Improvement Group/Civilization Class was founded by me, Davon McNeil, and patient Daryl Golston. This program is designed to promote self-awareness, self-worth, self- improvement and self-reformation. We're young men who, at one time in our lives, existed within a complete negative mental state and the consequences were long prison sentences. We made the conscious and responsible choice to change our lives for the better by isolating our minds and working rigorously on the psychological infrastructure which was the root cause of our behavior. We want to show other young men that positive change is readily available when an individual is truly sincere about changing their lives. Also, the Civilization Class is also a "do what you always did; get what you always got" approach which promotes self-worth, self-empowerment.

The Self-Improvement Group/Civilization Class was approved by Superintendent Veronica Madden and Director of Treatment James Riox. Our first group session was held on March 20, 2015.

The following is a formal proposal for the formulation and implementation of the Civilization Class Program at Bridgewater State Hospital (BSH) medium security facility in Bridgewater, Massachusetts.

Vision

We, as an anti-crime and mentally conscious people, can restore individuals back to stability and instill hope, with the goal of rehabilitating individuals. To provide them with some real life tools they can implement and use in their daily activities. This will give those the opportunity to experience making healthy choices which will in turn create healthy circumstances for themselves. This will ultimately lead to shaping healthy environments for the betterment of the commune (DOC Staff/Inmate relationship).

Mission

The mission is to isolate the mind and work vigorously on the psychological infrastructure which is the root cause of our behavior. Doing and/or adhering to some psychic readjustment will enable the group to grow collectively through individual analysis of the self. Building pro positive insights about civil competency and moral consciousness; disassociating from the negative precepts and concepts which breeds unhealthy thinking. This leads to dysfunctional and uncivilized behavior, thus distorting the reality of self and the community we abuse as a result.

Curriculum

This curriculum is outlined with the objective of offering each participant the opportunity to: 1) participate in discussion and self-awareness as to what it means to become civilized and what is the importance of this divine attribute; 2) to foster self-worth and build confidence in group members to become stronger members of a community; and 3) to be exposed to the inner- workings of the significant impact of the individual on the greater community.

Process

Over the course of a 9-week program, we will look at and analyze different aspects of the self, the community, mental illness, problem-solving and relevancy of respected principles learned and promoted by incarcerated men who made a conscious choice to grow and develop. Inmates and/or Patients who participate will be expected to show up on time; respect one another; no swearing; no sleeping; and must participate in group discussions as well as take notes.

Program Facilitators

The two inmate/patient program facilitators will assist with the distribution and collection of program materials. They will also be responsible for maintaining a written record of all program participant's names, topic(s) discussed and the agenda for the following week. These records will be available for review by BSH staff.

Operational Requirements

Operational requirements for the Civilization Class, i.e. copies, pens and pads, will be provided by BSH staff. BSH staff will have final approval of all materials used.

Meeting Space

The Civilization Class meetings will be held in an assigned classroom in the MID-MODS block decided by BSH staff. Assigned program time will be in addition to MID-MODS program offerings.

Scheduling

The program will be conducted twice, four times per month, and will be scheduled at dates and times determined by MID-MODS staff.

Summary

As I conclude, I will assure you that we remain optimistic about the joint endeavor of changing lives. The key facilitators have developed a working relationship which is transparent amongst the BSH community; by placing into motion the tools and rules needed to achieve said objective of "civilization"; and knowing that to further progress, opportunity must be exploited every time The proposal for the Civilization Class program is now officially submitted for your review and approval.

Respectfully,

Davon McNeil & Daryl Golston

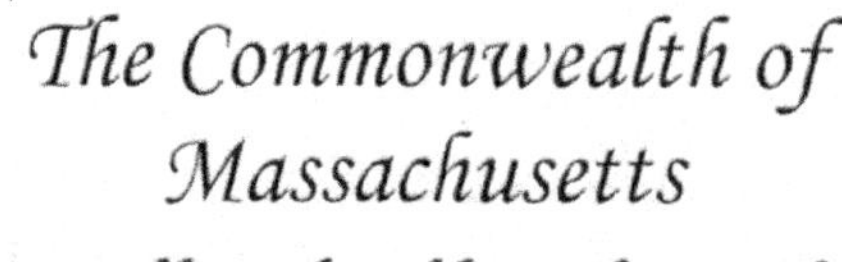

Executive Office of Public Safety and Security
Department of Correction
Bridgewater State Hospital
20 Administration Rd.
Bridgewater, Massachusetts 02324
(508) 279-4500
www.mass.gov/doc

August 9, 2015

Mr. Davon McNeill #W82395
Bridgewater State Hospital
20 Administration Road
Bridgewater, MA 02324

Dear Mr. McNeill,

I appreciate your letter of September 6, 2015, requesting I reconsider my failure to approve the "Choices" Program that you are seeking to start. I am a strong supporter of providing education and direction to youngsters in hopes of having them avoid the practices and behaviors that will lead to addiction, criminality, injuring others and not leading the full and happy lives they should. However, this is not the right time for this program at this facility. It may be some time in the future, but not at this time.

I do appreciate your creativity and concern and desire to do something positive and urge you to continue to pursue meaningful activities and programs and hope to hear from you with more ideas.

Sincerely,

Veronica M. Madden
Superintendent

VM/bjm
FRN 15-35

Cc: File

The Commonwealth of Massachusetts

Executive Office of Public Safety and Security

Department of Correction

Bridgewater State Hospital

20 Administration Rd.

Bridgewater, Massachusetts 02324

(508) 279-4500

www.mass.gov/doc

Charles D. Baker
Governor

Karyn Polito
Lieutenant Governor

Daniel Bennett
Secretary

Carol Higgins O'Brien
Commissioner

Katherine A. Chmiel
Thomas E. Dickhaut
Michael G. Grant
Deputy Commissioners

Daniel Calis
Superintendent

February 18, 2016

Mr. Davon McNeill #W82395
Bridgewater State Hospital
20 Administration Road
Bridgewater, MA 02324

Dear Mr. McNeill,

I reviewed your program proposal "Choices" you sent me on January 31, 2016. While I appreciate your vision with this program after careful consideration I don't think this program is appropriate for the population here at Bridgewater State Hospital at this time.

I applaud your positive ideas and encourage you to continue to create a better place to live for our youth.

Sincerely,

Daniel Calis
Superintendent

DC/bjm
FRN 16-12

Cc: File

The Setback

On August 6, 2015, I was housed at Bridgewater State Hospital (The Cadre Program). I was summoned to my case worker's office by the unit officer who informed me that someone from the Massachusetts Parole Office was there to serve me with my parole decision. I'd been waiting almost two months to receive that decision. Upon entering the office I was greeted by the case worker and a male representative. He shook my hand, told me his name and instructed me to have a seat. Once he confirmed I was Davon McNeil and after I stated my date of birth, he handed me four sheets of paper that were stapled together. He informed me that the Parole Board denied my parole with a review hearing in three years. To say that I was devastated is an understatement. As I sat there reading the decision, I began to feel fatigued. I just couldn't believe they denied my parole. In that moment, I felt drained of all energy and completely defeated. The guy from the parole office stated he was sorry for the upsetting news and left after he had me sign a few documents. The case worker asked me if I wanted to speak with someone from the mental health department, but I politely declined. At that very moment I felt that all of the hard work and positive institutional programming I was involved in was all for nothing. What was worse than the denial was me having to call home and tell my family that I wasn't coming home and all the plans we'd made were not going to happen. I knew for sure my fiancée and two daughters were going to be heartbroken and experience emotional pain when I told them about the three-year setback. They had been my major support system for the entire duration of my incarceration, investing a great amount of time, money and energy for me to come home. I made the phone call and surprisingly, they didn't take the news as hard as I imagined they would. In fact, they were more concerned about me and my mental state. My fiancée and two daughters encouraged me to stay strong and to remain focused on my positive growth and development. That's all I needed to hear to regain my mental, emotional and spiritual fortitude. I was about to embark on a mission to demonstrate my rehabilitation and positive institutional adjustment, as required by the Massachusetts Parole Board. I was determined to achieve my physical freedom. The following is a copy of my 2015 parole decision. Peace!

"The choices that we make will shape our lives forever!"

~ "Bronx Tale," the movie

The Commonwealth of Massachusetts
Executive Office of Public Safety and Security

PAROLE BOARD

12 Mercer Road
Natick, Massachusetts 01760

Telephone # (508) 650-4500
Facsimile # (508) 650-4599

Charles D. Baker
Governor

Karyn Polito
Lieutenant Governor

Daniel Bennett
Secretary

Charlene Bonner
Chairperson

DECISION

IN THE MATTER OF

DAVON MCNEIL

W82395

TYPE OF HEARING:	**Initial Hearing**
DATE OF HEARING:	**June 16, 2015**
DATE OF DECISION:	**August 5, 2015**

PARTICIPATING BOARD MEMBERS: Dr. Charlene Bonner, Tonomey Coleman, Sheila Dupre, Lee Gartenberg, Ina Howard-Hogan, Tina Hurley, Lucy Soto-Abbe.

DECISION OF THE BOARD: After careful consideration of all relevant facts, including the nature of the underlying offense, criminal record, institutional record, the inmate's testimony at the hearing, and the views of the public as expressed at the hearing or in written submissions to the Board, we conclude by unanimous vote that the inmate is not a suitable candidate for parole. Parole is denied with a review in three years from the date of the hearing.[1]

I. STATEMENT OF THE CASE

On September 15, 2003, after a jury trial in Plymouth Superior Court, Davon McNeil was found guilty of second degree murder and sentenced to life in prison. McNeil's conviction was affirmed in November 2006 (*Commonwealth v. McNeil*, 67 Mass. App. Ct. 1115 (2006)). In May 2007, the Supreme Judicial Court denied further appellate review (*Commonwealth v. McNeil*, 449 Mass. 1102 (2006)).

The facts of the case are as follows: On July 19, 2000, at approximately 12:30 pm, Brockton Police responded to a series of gunshots in the area of 30 Fuller Street. Upon arrival, police learned that all parties involved in the shooting had fled the area. Minutes later, police received information from the city hospital that a gunshot victim (later identified as Bruce Montrond) had just been brought to the emergency room. Mr. Montrond died as a result of two gunshot wounds; one to the chest and one to the abdomen.

After a thorough investigation into Mr. Montrond's murder, police determined that earlier in the day on July 19, Karen Lopes (Mr. Montrond's cousin) had given Mr. Montrond and a friend a ride to Fuller Street. Ms. Lopes had pulled over near 34 Fuller Street and Mr. Montrond and his friend then exited the car. At that time, McNeil was also walking on Fuller Street and he and Mr. Montrond began to have a verbal dispute. Ms. Lopes had remained in the car (facing away from the group), when she heard what sounded like gunshots coming from behind her. She turned and looked towards the noise and saw a black male with a gun, firing in the direction of Mr. Montrond. The shooter, later identified as McNeil, then ran to a white car parked in the driveway of 30 Fuller Street and drove away. Ms. Lopes then leaned over to open the front passenger door, as Mr. Montrond collapsed into her car. She then drove the victim to the hospital. When shown a photo array, Ms. Lopes identified Davon McNeil as the shooter. There were also several other individuals who witnessed the shooting and had identified McNeil as both the shooter and the person arguing with the victim before he was shot.

On July 24, 2000, 22-year-old McNeil was arrested in Dorchester and charged with the murder of 20-year-old Bruce Montrond.

II. PAROLE HEARING ON JUNE 16, 2015

McNeil is now 37-years old. This is his first appearance before the Parole Board and he was not represented by an attorney. McNeil has been incarcerated since 2000 and is currently serving his sentence at Bridgewater State Hospital (BSH), where he is an inmate Cadre worker.

McNeil began the hearing by offering an apology to the victim's family. He stated that he "selfishly shot and killed your son. I was a coward, savage, young punk who hid behind a 38 caliber. Bruce had nothing to do with my deep rooted anger. Bruce didn't do anything wrong. For this I beg your forgiveness. Please forgive me." McNeil then provided the Parole Board with pertinent information about his childhood and described how specific life experiences contributed to his poor decision making as a young man. McNeil recalls that as a young boy, his mother brought him to various correctional institutions to visit his father. He described how this affected him and his relationship with his mother. McNeil stated that he lived with various family members, where he received "a lot of love, but a lot of misguidance." He also stated that he smoked marijuana freely and witnessed his mother using crack cocaine. He said his family was very close and, although his grandparents provided a model of strong work ethic, he was exposed to a culture of gambling, drugs, hustling, and addiction throughout his daily life. McNeil reported that such destructive behavior was normal to him. McNeil was eventually introduced to his friend's older brother, who introduced McNeil to selling drugs. McNeil identified this introduction as the pinnacle of his criminal lifestyle. He told the Board that by age 12 or 13, he was selling crack cocaine.

McNeil stated that he progressed in the business of selling drugs, which supported the lifestyle of both him and his mother. As part of his drug sales, McNeil stated that he owned two guns. He said that despite his prior criminal convictions, he never had serious intentions of changing his lifestyle. McNeil stated that it was not until this sentence, did he begin to invest in changing his life and seriously reflect on what he had done.

McNeil detailed the precipitants and incidents that led to the shooting death of Bruce Montrond. His version of the murder was generally consistent with known facts. McNeil detailed the argument between himself and several friends in the days prior to the shooting, as well as the eventual escalation of events on the day of the murder. McNeil told parole staff (prior to this hearing) that he drew his gun because a friend of his yelled "he got a gun!" This was in reference to Mr. Montrond's friend, who was standing near Montrond and McNeil. Board Members pressed McNeil on his assertion that he fired only after his friend alerted him to the possibility that Mr. Montrond's friend had a gun. McNeil denied shooting in self-defense per-se, yet he made it clear that the fear he experienced of possibly being shot led him to "recklessly" fire his weapon. He said that he and his friend then jumped in their car and drove away. McNeil described a scenario in which he went to his grandmother's home in Dorchester and confessed to her. He said that he was immediately remorseful for what he had done. He stated that his grandmother encouraged him to turn himself in and to "leave it in God's hands." McNeil instead tried to flee, but was apprehended five days after the murder. He initially denied committing the offense when arrested by the police.

McNeil stated that in 2007, after "a culmination of things," he accepted full responsibility. He described looking at a picture of his daughter (who was two months old when he went to prison) and "my conscience began to wake up." He stated that was the first step in a process that led him to positive change. The second event that prompted him to change was learning that his mother lost her legs due to medical issues. He described her coming to visit him and how he realized that while incarcerated, he couldn't be there to help her with all of her needs. McNeil stated that he then began to internalize words his grandmother had told him when he was first incarcerated, as well as advice his father had given him, about making positive use of his time instead of choosing to continue on the path of self-destruction. McNeil stated that he also learned from the transformation his aunts had made in their own lives. He stated that he keeps a card posted on his cell wall from his aunt that reads "this will not be your legacy." He realizes now that he can lead a positive and productive life, and that he will never again hurt anyone.

The Board asked McNeil about the number and content of tattoos that he accumulated while incarcerated. He admitted that he did not have any tattoos before he came to prison, but in 2005, he decided to have the words "street certified" and "gangsta code" tattooed on his body. He agreed that such phrases illustrate a lack of positive rehabilitation and that in deciding to get such tattoos, he continued to have the mentality of a young man who glorified the criminal street life. McNeil now regrets having these tattoos and insists that his current values (gained through programming and rehabilitation) are in direct conflict with the person he once was.

McNeil provided the Board with a detailed history of his transformation and described the programs which provided him with the tools necessary to change his behavior and mentality. McNeil stated that the Correctional Recovery Academy was the most influential program he completed. McNeil was able to start a "self-improvement group" for patients suffering with mental illness at BSH. McNeil stated that being able to help those who struggle with talking about their own feelings has been a significant source of growth for him.

McNeil continued throughout the hearing to verbalize how far he has come on his path toward rehabilitation. He stated that although the bulk of his programming did not commence until 2010, his personal mission to change began in 2007. McNeil said that he has gained the necessary tools and desire to live a productive, law abiding life. He stated that he has the employment skills, the ambition, and a support system that will assist him with successful re-entry into the community.

McNeil had many supporters attend his hearing. Speaking in support of his parole were his father, the mother of his daughter, his aunt, a cousin, and a family friend. Each supporter provided their personal knowledge of McNeil's transformation and outlined how they will be able to assist him upon his release. He had one friend who stated that he will assist him financially, as well as with employment opportunities.

The mother of the victim spoke in opposition to McNeil's parole. She stated that "he destroyed my life." She said that her husband died soon after their son was murdered and that she attributes his death to the stress he endured as a direct result of the murder of their son. She described how the death of her son has impacted her life and how she has not been able to move beyond such a loss. Plymouth County Assistant District Attorney Suzanne McDonough testified against parole for McNeil and provided the Board with a letter in opposition from District Attorney Timothy Cruz.

III. DECISION

Davon McNeil appeared before the Parole Board for the first time after serving 15 years of his life sentence. Until 2005, McNeil had continued to value the street mentality that led to his criminal lifestyle, as demonstrated by his acquisition of tattoos glorifying such thinking. He admits that his internal transformation only began in 2007, followed by a recent investment in the core programs in 2010. However, McNeil appears to have made the commitment to genuinely invest in positive rehabilitation and he appears to be benefitting from his investment in programming. McNeil has worked his way into a Cadre position, where he helped develop a group for mentally ill inmates to share their feelings and experiences. The Parole Board recognizes that since 2010, McNeil has been working hard to reach the stage of rehabilitation that will enable him an opportunity to be successful in the community. However, he still has more work to do. A longer period of positive adjustment and continued rehabilitation is needed before McNeil meets the legal standard for parole.

The standard we apply in assessing candidates for parole is set out in 120 C.M.R. 300.04, which provides that "Parole Board Members shall only grant a parole permit if they are of the opinion that there is a reasonable probability that, if such offender is released, the offender will live and remain at liberty without violating the law and that release is not incompatible with the welfare of society." Applying that appropriately high standard here, it is the unanimous opinion of the Board that McNeil does not merit parole at this time. Parole is denied with a review in three years. The Parole Board will review McNeil's progress in three years, which will allow him adequate time to continue on his path of rehabilitation and to demonstrate a longer period of positive stability.

I certify that this is the decision and reasons of the Massachusetts Parole Board regarding the above referenced hearing. Pursuant to G.L. c. 127, § 130, I further certify that all voting Board Members have reviewed the applicant's entire criminal record. This signature does not indicate authorship of the decision.

Michael J. Callahan, General Counsel

August 5, 2015
Date

DAVON MCNEIL

The Victory

On February 6, 2019, I was housed at Old Colony Correctional Center when I was summoned to the institution's parole office by the unit officer. I knew within my heart that I was being summoned to receive my parole decision. I'd been waiting eight grueling moths for it to arrive. I was still traumatized from the results (denial) of my previous decision, so the three minute walk to the parole office was extremely stressful. Upon entering the office I was greeted by a lady from the Massachusetts Parole Office. She shook my hand, told me her name and wasted no time telling me that the Parole Board had given me a positive parole vote. She congratulated me for achieving a positive parole decision and for putting in the hard work. I asked her if I could sit down and read the decision and she told me, "Sure, take as long as you need." I couldn't hold back the tears of joy that escaped from my eyes. After 19 years of incarceration I was finally going home. What a great feeling! As soon as I got back to the unit, I called my family and told them that I was coming home. They were overcome with happiness and couldn't stop screaming and crying. For 12 years I worked hard to show and prove to the Parole Board that I was rehabilitated and ready to become a productive member of society–and the work I did finally paid off. My transition from negative to positive wasn't an easy task, but I knew it had to be done if I wanted a chance at physical freedom. The following documents are all of the positive institutional programming I completed and graduated from during my three-year setback. You'll also see a copy of my 2019 parole decision. Positive Education Always Creates Elevation; and that's Peace! To my enlightener, Allah Fu-Quan, "God, I wouldn't be the man I am today without your divine guidance." Thank U-God! Peace is the way of the righteous. All praise be to Allah (The Father).

"While continuing to learn, intensify your already intense desire at every moment.
Become addicted to the pursuit of truth; it is founded from wanting to definitely
escape from the stages of darkness and returning to divinity."

~ (Allah Fu-Quan)

The Commonwealth of Massachusetts
Executive Office of Public Safety and Security
PAROLE BOARD

12 Mercer Road
Natick, Massachusetts 01760

Telephone # (508) 650-4500
Facsimile # (508) 650-4599

DECISION

IN THE MATTER OF

DAVON MCNEIL

W82395

TYPE OF HEARING: **Review Hearing**

DATE OF HEARING: **June 26, 2018**

DATE OF DECISION: **February 21, 2019**

PARTICIPATING BOARD MEMBERS: Paul M. Treseler, Dr. Charlene Bonner, Tonomey Coleman, Sheila Dupre, Tina Hurley, Colette Santa, Lucy Soto-Abbe

DECISION OF THE BOARD: After careful consideration of all relevant facts, including the nature of the underlying offense, criminal record, institutional record, the inmate's testimony at the hearing, and the views of the public as expressed at the hearing or in written submissions to the Board, we conclude by unanimous vote that the inmate is a suitable candidate for parole. Parole is granted to an approved home plan after 18 months in lower security and with special conditions.

I. STATEMENT OF THE CASE

On September 15, 2003, after a jury trial in Plymouth Superior Court, Davon McNeil was found guilty of second degree murder for the death of Bruce Montrond and sentenced to serve life in prison with the possibility of parole. Mr. McNeil's conviction was affirmed in November 2006 (*Commonwealth v. McNeil*, 67 Mass. App. Ct. 1115 (2006)). In May 2007, the Supreme Judicial Court denied further appellate review (*Commonwealth v. McNeil*, 449 Mass. 1102 (2006)).

On July 19, 2000, at approximately 12:30 p.m., Brockton police responded to a series of gunshots in the area of 30 Fuller Street. Upon arrival, police learned that all parties involved in the shooting had fled the area. Minutes later, police received information from the city hospital that a gunshot victim (later identified as Bruce Montrond) had just been brought to the emergency room. Mr. Montrond died as a result of two gunshot wounds: one to the chest and one to the abdomen.

After a thorough investigation, police determined that earlier in the day on July 19, Mr. Montrond's cousin had given him and his friend a ride to Fuller Street, where they exited the car. Mr. McNeil was also walking on Fuller Street, and he and Mr. Montrond began to have a verbal dispute. Mr. Montrond's cousin remained in the car and heard gunshots coming from behind her. She saw a black male with a gun, firing in the direction of Mr. Montrond. The shooter, later identified as Mr. McNeil, then ran to a car and drove away. Mr. Montrond's cousin then leaned over to open the front passenger door, as Mr. Montrond collapsed into her car. She drove him to the hospital. When shown a photo array, Mr. Montrond's cousin identified Mr. McNeil as the shooter. There were also several other individuals who witnessed the shooting and had identified Mr. McNeil as the shooter, as well as the person arguing with the victim before he was shot. On July 24, 2000, 22-year-old Davon McNeil was arrested in Dorchester and charged with the murder of 20-year-old Bruce Montrond.

II. PAROLE HEARING ON JUNE 26, 2018

Davon McNeil, now 41-years-old, appeared before the Parole Board on June 26, 2018, for a review hearing. Mr. McNeil was represented by Student Attorneys Alexandra Rawlings and Milo Inglehart of the Harvard Prison Legal Assistance Project. Mr. McNeil had been denied parole after his initial hearing in 2015. Mr. McNeil offered an apology to the victim's family, as well as apologies to his own family and neighborhood for the damage his actions caused. Mr. McNeil admitted that he was a drug dealer, who was completely immersed in the "street lifestyle" starting at age 15. He acknowledged that the absence of his incarcerated father and the substance abuse of his mother led to him leave home and engage in activities that contributed to the destruction of his neighborhood.

The Board questioned Mr. McNeil as to how he would characterize the governing offense. He said that he committed a senseless murder because he was an angry, selfish person with no control of his emotions. He told the Board that he had known Mr. McNeil to be a good, loyal person with a loving family, who did not deserve what he did. Mr. McNeil said that since his incarceration, and specifically since his initial hearing in 2015, he has done his best to remedy his shortcomings through programming. The Board noted Mr. McNeil's lack of disciplinary issues in prison and asked how he succeeded in staying out of trouble. Mr. McNeil stated that he was determined to remove himself from the criminal lifestyle that led to the commission of the governing offense and, instead, chose to serve his time by "focus[ing] on becoming a better person."

Mr. McNeil attributed his productivity in prison to his participation in programs, such as Advanced Anger Management, Restorative Justice, the Nurturing Fatherhood Program, and Project Youth, among others. Through these programs, Mr. McNeil explained that he finally began to understand the "deep ripple effect" of his crime. The Board further noted that Mr. McNeil has maintained employment and published two books throughout his incarceration. Mr. McNeil detailed a parole plan that consisted of a step down to minimum security, before being moved to a pre-release program that would allow him to work and save money to support both himself and his family. The Board noted Mr. McNeil's extensive family and community support, including his two daughters and a girlfriend of 25 years, with whom he would like to live, if granted parole. Mr. McNeil admitted that he could benefit from mental health counseling to assist with reentry after 18 years of incarceration.

Mr. McNeil's father, cousin, and a family friend testified in support of parole. The Board considered written submissions in support of parole from Mr. McNeil's girlfriend, five family members, a family friend, and three individuals involved in community programming. The victim's mother testified in opposition to parole. Plymouth County Assistant District Attorney Christina Crowley testified in opposition to parole. The Board also considered the written submission of Plymouth County District Attorney Timothy Cruz in opposition to parole.

III. DECISION

The Board is of the opinion that Davon McNeil has demonstrated a level of rehabilitative progress that would make his release compatible with the welfare of society.

The applicable standard used by the Board to assess a candidate for parole is: "Parole Board Members shall only grant a parole permit if they are of the opinion that there is a reasonable probability that, if such offender is released, the offender will live and remain at liberty without violating the law and that release is not incompatible with the welfare of society." 120 C.M.R. 300.04. In forming this opinion, the Board has taken consideration Mr. McNeil's institutional behavior, as well as his participation in available work, educational, and treatment programs during the period of his incarceration. The Board also considered a risk and needs assessment and whether risk reduction could effectively minimize Mr. McNeil's risk of recidivism. After applying this appropriately high standard to the circumstances of Mr. McNeil's case, the Board is of the opinion that Davon McNeil merits parole at this time. Parole is granted to an approved home plan after 18 months in lower security and with special conditions.

SPECIAL CONDITIONS: Approve home plan before release; Waive work for two weeks; Must be at home between 10 pm and 6 am at PO's discretion; Electronic monitoring - GPS at PO's discretion; Supervise for drugs, testing in accordance with agency policy; Supervise for liquor abstinence, testing in accordance with agency policy; Report to assigned MA Parole Office on day of release; No contact with victim's family; Must have substance abuse evaluation and adhere to plan; Must have mental health counseling and adhere to plan.

I certify that this is the decision and reasons of the Massachusetts Parole Board regarding the above referenced hearing. Pursuant to G.L. c. 127, § 130, I further certify that all voting Board Members have reviewed the applicant's entire criminal record. This signature does not indicate authorship of the decision.

Shara Benedetti, Acting General Counsel

2/21/19
Date

My D-Report History

The following documents are copies of the eleven disciplinary reports that I have accumulated during my 19 years of incarceration. As you'll see, the majority of them were issued for minor infractions. The acquiring of D-Reports is a practice I strived to shy away from at all costs. My sole objective was always to liberate myself from the confines of prison, not remain within its jaws; and incurring frivolous disciplinary reports would have certainly put stumbling blocks along my path of freedom. Peace!

"We may encounter many defeats, but we must not be defeated."

~ Maya Angelou

COMMONWEALTH OF MASSACHUSETTS
DEPARTMENT OF CORRECTION
DISCIPLINARY REPORT

Inmate MCNEIL, DAVON **Commit No** W82395 **Location** *NEW LINE

Date 20031219 **D- Report No** 29333 **Institution** MCI CONCORD

Category	Offense(s)
5	5/1/DISOBEYING AN ORDER, LYING, INSOLENCE
5	5/2/VIOLATING ANY DEPARTMENT RULE OR REGULATION
5	5/8/CONDUCT WHICH DISRUPTS

Description of Offense(s

On December 19 , 2003 at aproximately 6:15pm I ,CO Haskell ,assigned to New Line Up was approached by inmate Davon McNeil, W82395 cell 34 ,stating he would refuse to lock in his cell when requested to by this reporting officer.At this time proper authourities were notified of incident.

Inmate Mcneil was subsequently place in restraints and escorted to HSU by Lt. Jaworski and CO Merlino to be seen by medical staff and was placed in a holding cell.

Disciplinary Report Type: Major

Has Inmate been placed on Awaiting Action Status Yes [] No [X]

Referred to DA [] Yes [X] No **Referred to DDU** [] Yes [X] No

Reporting Staff Frederick R Haskell **Date** 20031219 **Time** 18:53

Days off Wed Thu

Shift 3-11

Supervisor ______ **Date** ______ **Time** ______

Shift Commander Paul J Aucoin **Date** 20031219 **Time** 22:10

Disciplinary Officer Brien C Durkee **Date** 20031220 **Time** 13:30

Results PLEA GUILTY

Continuance Length ______ **Continuance Date** 20031222 **Projected Date** ______

Offenses	Sanctions	Start Date	Unit	#of Units	Credits	End Date	Amount
5/1/DISOBEYING AN ORDER, LYING, INSOLENCE	Loss Canteen	20040106	D	28		20040203	
5/2/VIOLATING ANY DEPARTMENT RULE OR REGULATION	Loss Telephone	20040106	D	28		20040203	
5/8/CONDUCT WHICH DISRUPTS	Loss Visits	20040106	D	28		20040203	

Reviewing Authority Peter St. Amand **Date** 20031222 **Time** 12:30

20181212 11:58

DAVON MCNEIL

COMMONWEALTH OF MASSACHUSETTS
DEPARTMENT OF CORRECTION
DISCIPLINARY REPORT

Inmate MCNEIL, DAVON **Commit No** W82395 **Location** M2

Date 20050327 **D- Report No** 53522 **Institution** SOUZA-BARANOWSKI CORRECTIONAL

Offenses	Sanctions	Start Date	Unit	#of Units	Credits	End Date	Amount
INSOLENCE							
5/13/GAMBLING	Loss Canteen	20050401	D	14		20050415	
5/2/VIOLATING ANY DEPARTMENT RULE OR REGULATION	Loss of Yard		D	30			
5/33/ATTEMPTING TO COMMIT ANY OFFENSE	Not Guilty						

Reviewing Authority Thomas E Dickhaut **Date** 20050425 **Time** 15:15

20181212 11:57

COMMONWEALTH OF MASSACHUSETTS
DEPARTMENT OF CORRECTION
DISCIPLINARY REPORT

Inmate MCNEIL, DAVON **Commit No** W82395 **Location** N2

Date 20060310 **D- Report No** 72723 **Institution** SOUZA-BARANOWSKI CORRECTIONAL

Category	Offense(s)
3	3/01/Lying to or providing false information to a staff member
3	3/14/Giving, selling, borrowing, lending, or trading money or anything of value to, or accepting or purchasing money or anything of value from another inmate or an inmate?s friend(s) or family

Description of Offense(s

Following an investigation into the suspected improper disbursement of inmate funds, it has been determined that inmate Mcneil, Davon W82395 did use a third party outside of Souza-Baranowski Correctional Center to send money to inmate Shawn Hart W83876 who is incarcerated at Souza-Baranowski Correctional Center. Inmate Mcneil did send money to Ms Barbara Stevenson for the amount of thirty dollars. It should be noted that three other inmates also sent Barbara Stevenson money totaling eighty dollars. Inmate Shawn Hart subsequently received a money order from Barbara Stevenson for the total of one hundred and ten dollars. While interviewing inmate Mcneil he stated that Ms Stevenson was a dog breeder on the streets and that he and his brother did buy two dogs from her. Inmate Mcneil sent thirty dollars to her to pay for the vaccinations for the dogs.

Through interviewing inmate Shawn Hart who is housed at Souza-Baranowski Correctional Center inmate Hart stated that Barbara Stevenson is his grandmother. This officer questioned Shawn Hart and asked if she (Barbara Stevenson) was a dog breeder and he said no. Inmate Hart stated that he did not know who inmate Mcneil was. Inmate Mcneil did lie to this reporting officer regarding the reason for sending the money out.

Inmate Mcneil was notified that he would be receiving a disciplinary report for this incident.

Disciplinary Report Type: Formal

Has Inmate been placed on Awaiting Action Status **Yes** [X] **No** [ ]

Referred to DA [ ] **Yes** [X] **No** **Referred to DDU** [ ] **Yes** [X] **No**

Reporting Staff Kevin P Shepard **Date** 20060310 **Time** 11:31

Days off Sun Mon

Shift flex

Supervisor Nestor L Cruz **Date** 20060310 **Time** 11:34

Shift Commander Robert J Blood **Date** 20060310 **Time** 11:56

Disciplinary Officer James R Hart **Date** 20060313 **Time** 13:33

Results Continuance without a Finding

Continuance Length 30 Days **Continuance Date** 20060317 **Projected Date** 20060519

Offenses	Sanctions	Start Date	Unit	#of Units	Credits	End Date	Amount
3/01/Lying to or providing false information to a staff member	NONE						0
3/14/Giving, selling, borrowing, lending, or trading money or anything of	Loss Canteen		D	60			0

20181212 11:57

DAVON MCNEIL

COMMONWEALTH OF MASSACHUSETTS
DEPARTMENT OF CORRECTION
DISCIPLINARY REPORT

Inmate MCNEIL, DAVON **Commit No** W82395 **Location** N2

Date 20060310 **D- Report No** 72723 **Institution** SOUZA-BARANOWSKI CORRECTIONAL

Offenses	Sanctions	Start Date	Unit	#of Units	Credits	End Date	Amount
value to, or accepting or purchasing money or anything of value from another inmate or an inmate?s friend(s) or family							

Reviewing Authority Duane MacEachern **Date** 20060420 **Time** 11:04

20181212 11:57

COMMONWEALTH OF MASSACHUSETTS
DEPARTMENT OF CORRECTION
DISCIPLINARY REPORT

Inmate MCNEIL, DAVON **Commit No** W82395 **Location** Unit Team Captain

Date 20070610 **D- Report No** 107871 **Institution** OLD COLONY CORRECTIONAL CENTER

Category	Offense(s)
4	4/01/Receipt or possession of contraband
4	4/14/*Possession of an altered appliance

Description of Offense(s

On June 10, 2007, at appproximately 8:45, a search was conducted of cell G-23 in the Dawes Two Housing Unit Inmate Davon Mcneil was found to be in possion of an altered hot pot (bypass wire) which was confiscated and secured as evidance.

Disciplinary Report Type: Formal

Has Inmate been placed on Awaiting Action Status Yes [ ] No [X]

Referred to DA [ ] Yes [X] No **Referred to DDU** [ ] Yes [X] No

Reporting Staff Dean W Hardy **Date** 20070610 **Time** 22:15

Days off Wed Thu

Shift 3x11

Supervisor Stephen A Kennedy **Date** 20070610 **Time** 22:17

Shift Commander Kenneth J Ayala **Date** 20070610 **Time** 22:17

Disciplinary Officer David W Malone **Date** 20070611 **Time** 07:22

Results Continuance without a Finding

Continuance Length 30 Days **Continuance Date** 20070613 **Projected Date** 20070714

Offenses	Sanctions	Start Date	Unit	#of Units	Credits	End Date	Amount
4/01/Receipt or possession of contraband	Dismissed		D				0
4/14/*Possession of an altered appliance	Loss Canteen		D	7	0		0

Reviewing Authority ______ **Date** ______ **Time** ______

20181212 11:57

COMMONWEALTH OF MASSACHUSETTS
DEPARTMENT OF CORRECTION
DISCIPLINARY REPORT

Inmate MCNEIL, DAVON **Commit No** W82395 **Location** D2

Date 20071204 **D- Report No** 121236 **Institution** OLD COLONY CORRECTIONAL CENTER

Category	Offense(s)
3	3/20/*Being tattooed while incarcerated, tattooing another, or possessing tattoo paraphernalia and/or body piercing
4	4/01/Receipt or possession of contraband
4	4/11/Violating any departmental rule or regulation, or any other rule, regulation, or condition of an institution or community based program

Description of Offense(s

On Tuesday December 4, 2007 inmate McNeil, Davon W 82395 was found to have violated Department Rules and Regulations. While conducting a search of cell G-23 I C/O Mike Carton IPS and IPS John Semedo did find the following contraband. 1 Tattoo needle and 1 altered hot pot. Upon searching McNeil he was found to have a new tattoo on his left forearm that read "Black Angel". He was found to have 5 other tattoos on his arms and chest that were not documented in IMS. He was seen by Medical and photo's were taken. Inmate McNeil was placed on A/A and all notifications were made.

Disciplinary Report Type: Formal

Has Inmate been placed on Awaiting Action Status **Yes** [X] **No** [ ]

Referred to DA [ ] **Yes** [X] **No** **Referred to DDU** [ ] **Yes** [X] **No**

Reporting Staff Michael D Carton **Date** 20071204 **Time** 21:17

Days off Fri Sat

Shift 2-10

Supervisor William N Slavick **Date** 20071204 **Time** 21:25

Shift Commander William J Grossi **Date** 20071204 **Time** 21:45

Disciplinary Officer John R Poulin **Date** 20071205 **Time** 07:30

Results PLEA GUILTY

Continuance Length ________ **Continuance Date** 20071210 **Projected Date** ________

Offenses	Sanctions	Start Date	Unit	#of Units	Credits	End Date	Amount
3/20/*Being tattooed while incarcerated, tattooing another, or possessing tattoo paraphernalia and/or body piercing	Restitution	20080115	D	15		20080201	15
	Loss Canteen	20080115	D	30	0	20080214	0
4/01/Receipt or possession of contraband	Dismissed		D				0
4/11/Violating any departmental rule or regulation, or any other rule, regulation, or condition of an	Dismissed		D				0

20181212 11:56

COMMONWEALTH OF MASSACHUSETTS
DEPARTMENT OF CORRECTION
DISCIPLINARY REPORT

Inmate MCNEIL, DAVON **Commit No** W82395 **Location** D2

Date 20071204 **D- Report No** 121236 **Institution** OLD COLONY CORRECTIONAL CENTER

Offenses	Sanctions	Start Date	Unit	#of Units	Credits	End Date	Amount
institution or community based program							

Reviewing Authority David J Kenneally **Date** 20080327 **Time** 10:22

20181212 11:56

DAVON MCNEIL

COMMONWEALTH OF MASSACHUSETTS
DEPARTMENT OF CORRECTION
DISCIPLINARY REPORT

Inmate MCNEIL, DAVON **Commit No** W82395 **Location** D2

Date 20081213 **D- Report No** 150183 **Institution** OLD COLONY CORRECTIONAL CENTER

Category	Offense(s)
3	3/10/Theft of property or possession of stolen property
4	4/01/Receipt or possession of contraband

Description of Offense(s

On Saturday December 13, 2008 at approximately 7:30 p.m., I CO O'Shaughnessy did find Inmate Davon McNeil W82395 to be in violation of department rules and regulations.

While conducting a search in the Dawes 2 cell G23 housing Inmates McNeil and inmate Michael Grinkley W87017, this officer did confiscate approximately 24 ounces of oatmeal wrapped in a clear plastic wrap. This officer also confiscated 12 individually wrapped pieces of what appeared to be laffy taffy in a 'Keefes Kitchen' rice bag. Inmate McNeil did admit to this officer that the items in question did belong to him and stated that they were actually lollipops. All items were confiscated and secured. All proper authorities.notified.

Disciplinary Report Type: Formal

Has Inmate been placed on Awaiting Action Status **Yes** [X] **No** [ ]

Referred to DA [ ] **Yes** [X] **No** **Referred to DDU** [ ] **Yes** [X] **No**

Reporting Staff Colin W O'Shaughnessy **Date** 20081213 **Time** 20:28

Days off Tue Wed

Shift 1X9

Supervisor Corey K Cotta **Date** 20081213 **Time** 20:40

Shift Commander William J Grossi **Date** 20081213 **Time** 20:52

Disciplinary Officer John R Poulin **Date** 20081214 **Time** 09:22

Results PLEA GUILTY

Continuance Length ______ **Continuance Date** 20081229 **Projected Date** ______

Offenses	Sanctions	Start Date	Unit	#of Units	Credits	End Date	Amount
3/10/Theft of property or possession of stolen property	Loss Canteen	20090120	D	14	0	20090203	0
4/01/Receipt or possession of contraband	Dismissed		D				0

Reviewing Authority David J Kenneally **Date** 20100402 **Time** 08:41

20181212 11:56

COMMONWEALTH OF MASSACHUSETTS
DEPARTMENT OF CORRECTION
DISCIPLINARY REPORT

Inmate MCNEIL, DAVON **Commit No** W82395 **Location** D1

Date 20090121 **D- Report No** 153164 **Institution** OLD COLONY CORRECTIONAL CENTER

Category	Offense(s)
3	3/14/Giving, selling, borrowing, lending, or trading money or anything of value to, or accepting or purchasing money or anything of value from another inmate or an inmate?s friend(s) or family
4	4/01/Receipt or possession of contraband
4	4/11/Violating any departmental rule or regulation, or any other rule, regulation, or condition of an institution or community based program
4	4/14/*Possession of an altered appliance

Description of Offense(s

On 1-21-09 at approximately 10:00 a.m. inmate Davon Mcneil W-82395 was in possession of a boiling hot pot which melted down and disrupted the institution.

While in Dawes 1 conducting a shakedown the smell of burning plastic was detected. As I Sergeant Marquis was walking down the lower right tier I observed smoke coming from cell G-23. I immediately notified Captain Gorden, who was in charge of the search, and the melted pot was unplugged and carried out to the courtyard. The unit did not have to be evacuated due to it being empty for the search.

After the search was completed a grievance round was conducted at that time inmate Mcneil stated that the hot pot was not his. He said it was left to him by another inmate. Upper Control and Shift Commander notified.

Disciplinary Report Type: Formal

Has Inmate been placed on Awaiting Action Status **Yes** [ ] **No** [X]

Referred to DA [ ] **Yes** [X] **No** **Referred to DDU** [ ] **Yes** [X] **No**

Reporting Staff Raymond J Marquis **Date** 20090121 **Time** 11:45

Days off Sun Sat

Shift 7-3

Supervisor Scott G Mello **Date** 20090121 **Time** 13:46

Shift Commander Peter L Pascucci **Date** 20090121 **Time** 13:46

Disciplinary Officer John R Poulin **Date** 20090121 **Time** 14:42

Results GUILTY

Continuance Length ______ **Continuance Date** 20090128 **Projected Date** ______

Offenses	Sanctions	Start Date	Unit	#of Units	Credits	End Date	Amount
3/14/Giving, selling, borrowing, lending, or trading money or anything of value to, or accepting or purchasing money or anything of value from another inmate or an inmate?s friend(s) or family	Dismissed		D				0

20181212 11:56

COMMONWEALTH OF MASSACHUSETTS
DEPARTMENT OF CORRECTION
DISCIPLINARY REPORT

Inmate MCNEIL, DAVON **Commit No** W82395 **Location** D1

Date 20090121 **D- Report No** 153164 **Institution** OLD COLONY CORRECTIONAL CENTER

Offenses	Sanctions	Start Date	Unit	#of Units	Credits	End Date	Amount
4/01/Receipt or possession of contraband	Dismissed		D				0
4/11/Violating any departmental rule or regulation, or any other rule, regulation, or condition of an institution or community based program	Dismissed		D				0
4/14/*Possession of an altered appliance	Loss of Hot Pot	20090217	D	21	0	20090310	0

Reviewing Authority David J Kenneally **Date** 20100406 **Time** 09:05

20181212 11:56

COMMONWEALTH OF MASSACHUSETTS
DEPARTMENT OF CORRECTION
DISCIPLINARY REPORT

Inmate MCNEIL, DAVON **Commit No** W82395 **Location** Mental Health Suite

Date 20090408 **D- Report No** 159665 **Institution** OLD COLONY CORRECTIONAL CENTER

Category	Offense(s)
2	2/23/Counterfeiting, committing forgery, altering or unauthorized reproduction of any document, article of identification, money, security, or official paper
2	2/29/*Attempting to commit any of the above offenses, making plans to commit any of the above offenses or aiding another person to commit any of the above offenses shall be considered the same as the commission of the offense itself
3	3/01/Lying to or providing false information to a staff member
3	3/29/*Attempting to commit any of the above offenses, making plans to commit any of the above offenses or aiding another person to commit any of the above offenses shall be considered the same as the commission of the offense itself
4	4/11/Violating any departmental rule or regulation, or any other rule, regulation, or condition of an institution or community based program
4	4/15/Attempting to commit any of the above offenses, making plans to commit any of the above offenses or aiding another person to commit any of the above offenses shall be considered the same as the commission of the offense itself

Description of Offense(s

On 4/8/09 at approximately 11:00 am I Sgt. Mark Fogaren interviewed inmate Davon McNeil W82395 regarding a grievance that he had filed regarding classroom space. This grievance was on a typed grievance from inwhich inmate McNeil had signed his name to. Inmate McNeil was asked questions regarding the contents of this grievanc and he could not answer any of the questions regarding the contents of said grievance. He states in the grievance that he had spoken directly to Director of Treatment Jeanne Lahousee it was determined that he had not spoken to her recently regarding this grievance contents. Inmate McNeil also admitted during the interview that he did not author said greivance but that it was handed to him and he was told to just sign his name to it. It should be noted that I did receive several what appears to be photocopied grievances inwhich the inmates had no knowledge of there contents and just signed their names to them. Inmate McNeil clearly violated the 103 CMR 491 grievance policy. All proper authorities were notified.

Disciplinary Report Type: Formal

Has Inmate been placed on Awaiting Action Status Yes [ ] No [X]

Referred to DA [ ] Yes [X] No **Referred to DDU** [ ] Yes [X] No

Reporting Staff Mark S Fogaren **Date** 20090408 **Time** 11:39

Days off Sun Sat

Shift 7-3

Supervisor Jeffrey R Souza **Date** 20090409 **Time** 14:05

Shift Commander Peter L Pascucci **Date** 20090409 **Time** 15:07

Disciplinary Officer Debra A Henriques **Date** 20090410 **Time** 08:10

Results Continuance without a Finding

Continuance Length 30 Days **Continuance Date** 20090427 **Projected Date** 20090527

20181212 11:55

DAVON MCNEIL

COMMONWEALTH OF MASSACHUSETTS
DEPARTMENT OF CORRECTION
DISCIPLINARY REPORT

Inmate MCNEIL, DAVON **Commit No** W82395 **Location** Mental Health Suite

Date 20090408 **D- Report No** 159665 **Institution** OLD COLONY CORRECTIONAL CENTER

Offenses	Sanctions	Start Date	Unit	#of Units	Credits	End Date	Amount
2/23/Counterfeiting, committing forgery, altering or unauthorized reproduction of any document, article of identification, money, security, or official paper	Dismissed		D				0
2/29/*Attempting to commit any of the above offenses, making plans to commit any of the above offenses or aiding another person to commit any of the above offenses shall be considered the same as the commission of the offense itself	Dismissed		D				0
3/01/Lying to or providing false information to a staff member	Dismissed		D				0
3/29/*Attempting to commit any of the above offenses, making plans to commit any of the above offenses or aiding another person to commit any of the above offenses shall be considered the same as the commission of the offense itself	Dismissed		D				0
4/11/Violating any departmental rule or regulation, or any other rule, regulation, or condition of an institution or community based program	Loss Canteen		D	14	0		0
4/15/Attempting to commit any of the above offenses, making plans to commit any of the above offenses or aiding another person to commit any of the above offenses shall be considered the same as the commission of the offense itself	Dismissed		D				0

Reviewing Authority David J Kenneally **Date** 20100416 **Time** 09:44

20181212 11:55

COMMONWEALTH OF MASSACHUSETTS
DEPARTMENT OF CORRECTION
DISCIPLINARY REPORT

Inmate MCNEIL, DAVON **Commit No** W82395 **Location** D2

Date 20090423 **D- Report No** 160788 **Institution** OLD COLONY CORRECTIONAL CENTER

Category	Offense(s)
3	3/14/Giving, selling, borrowing, lending, or trading money or anything of value to, or accepting or purchasing money or anything of value from another inmate or an inmate?s friend(s) or family
4	4/01/Receipt or possession of contraband
4	4/11/Violating any departmental rule or regulation, or any other rule, regulation, or condition of an institution or community based program

Description of Offense(s

On Thursday, April 23, 2009 at approximately 1730 I, CO David Hawkins while conducting a schedule search via IMS in Cell G23 of Dawes 2 did confiscate Hot Pot #570029 engraved with Inmate Dymond, Shawn (W90256), who has been released, that was in possession by Inmate McNeil, Davon (W82395) by his on admission. Lt. Fuller and Upper Control notified.

Disciplinary Report Type: Formal

Has Inmate been placed on Awaiting Action Status Yes [ ] No [X]

Referred to DA [ ] Yes [X] No **Referred to DDU** [ ] Yes [X] No

Reporting Staff David L Hawkins **Date** 20090423 **Time** 17:57

Days off Mon Tue

Shift 3x11

Supervisor Jason A Fuller **Date** 20090423 **Time** 20:12

Shift Commander Kenneth J Ayala **Date** 20090423 **Time** 21:21

Disciplinary Officer John R Poulin **Date** 20090424 **Time** 08:06

Results Continuance without a Finding

Continuance Length 30 Days **Continuance Date** 20090430 **Projected Date** 20090530

Offenses	Sanctions	Start Date	Unit	#of Units	Credits	End Date	Amount
3/14/Giving, selling, borrowing, lending, or trading money or anything of value to, or accepting or purchasing money or anything of value from another inmate or an inmate?s friend(s) or family	No Appliance		M	3	0		0
4/01/Receipt or possession of contraband	Dismissed		D				0
4/11/Violating any departmental rule or regulation, or any other rule,	Dismissed		D				0

20181212 11:55

COMMONWEALTH OF MASSACHUSETTS

DEPARTMENT OF CORRECTION

DISCIPLINARY REPORT

Inmate MCNEIL, DAVON **Commit No** W82395 **Location** D2

Date 20090423 **D- Report No** 160788 **Institution** OLD COLONY CORRECTIONAL CENTER

Offenses	Sanctions	Start Date	Unit	#of Units	Credits	End Date	Amount
regulation, or condition of an institution or community based program							

Reviewing Authority David J Kenneally **Date** 20100422 **Time** 07:55

20181212 11:55

COMMONWEALTH OF MASSACHUSETTS
DEPARTMENT OF CORRECTION
DISCIPLINARY REPORT

Inmate MCNEIL, DAVON **Commit No** W82395 **Location** C-2

Date 20110316 **D- Report No** 222552 **Institution** MCI SHIRLEY (MEDIUM)

Category	Offense(s)
3	3/01/Lying to or providing false information to a staff member
3	3/10/Theft of property or possession of stolen property
3	3/28/Possession of an altered appliance
4	4/01/Receipt or possession of contraband
4	4/02/Mutilating, defacing or destroying state property or the property of another person
4	4/14/*Possession of an altered appliance

Description of Offense(s

On the 3-16-11 at approximately 930am. I CO Brodmerkle while conducting a scheduled search of cell # 22 did find a hot pot that had the W number scratched off. Which was found on the desk. At this time I spoke with Inmate McNiel, Davon W82395 residing in 22., he denied knowing anything about the contriband hot pot. The hot pot was brought to property. Sgt Griffin notified.

Disciplinary Report Type: Formal

Has Inmate been placed on Awaiting Action Status Yes [ ] No [X]

Referred to DA [ ] Yes [X] No **Referred to DDU** [ ] Yes [X] No

Reporting Staff Robert A Brodmerkle **Date** 20110316 **Time** 10:41

Days off Fri Sat

Shift 1st

Supervisor Joseph A Cregg **Date** 20110316 **Time** 10:54

Shift Commander Thomas J Quinlivan **Date** 20110316 **Time** 10:54

Disciplinary Officer Thomas K Fedele **Date** 20110317 **Time** 07:01

Results DISMISSED

Continuance Length ______ **Continuance Date** ______ **Projected Date** ______

Reviewing Authority ______ **Date** ______ **Time** ______

20181212 11:55

DAVON MCNEIL

COMMONWEALTH OF MASSACHUSETTS
DEPARTMENT OF CORRECTION
DISCIPLINARY REPORT

Inmate MCNEIL, DAVON **Commit No** W82395 **Location** RU (RECOVERY UNIT)

Date 20170720 **D- Report No** 392440 **Institution** OLD COLONY CORRECTIONAL CENTER

Category	**Offense(s)**
3	3/01/Lying to or providing false information to a staff member
3	3/05/Refusing a direct order by any staff member
3	3/24/Being out of place or in an unauthorized area outside of the inmate's unit
3	3/26/Use of obscene, abusive or insolent language or gesture
3	3/27/Conduct which disrupts the normal operation of the facility or unit
3	3/30/Attempting to commit any of the above offenses, making plans to commit any of the above offenses or aiding another person to commit any of the above offenses shall be considered the same as the commission of the offense itself
4	4/11/Violating any departmental rule or regulation, or any other rule, regulation, or condition of an institution or community based program

Description of Offense(s

On Thursday July 20, 2017 it has been determined by this reporting Sergeant that inmate Davon McNeil W82395 did violate departmental rules and regulations by being out of place, being inappropriate with a female contract employee, and refusing a directive to assist with another patient in the Recovery Unit.
On Tuesday July 11, 2017 inmate Davon McNeil W82395 who is assigned to a companion in the Recovery Unit reported to the RU but the patient he was assigned to was at an outside hospital. Inmate McNeil instead of assisting with other patients took it upon himself to have a personal conversation with an RTA for a period of one hour. McNeil during the conversation with the RTA was informed by Mental Health clinician Penney that another patient in the RU was having a difficult time on the unit and requesting to speak with a companion but he refused the directive to assist the patient and continued to speak of personal issues with the RTA. McNeil when questioned about the hour long conversation with the RTA he alleged that he was speaking with the RTA regarding the companion program and also denied being asked to assist with another patient. McNeil?s purpose in the companion program is to assist with patients in the unit and not to speak of personal matters with a staff member. On July 13, 2017 McNeil was placed on AA/PI in Segregation.

Disciplinary Report Type: Formal

Has Inmate been placed on Awaiting Action Status **Yes** [ ] **No** [X]

Referred to DA [ ] **Yes** [X] **No** **Referred to DDU** [ ] **Yes** [X] **No**

Reporting Staff Dennis W Butler **Date** 20170720 **Time** 14:47

Days off Sun Sat

Shift 7-3

Supervisor Michael B Cunha **Date** 20170720 **Time** 14:50

Shift Commander David J Kenneally **Date** 20170720 **Time** 14:50

Disciplinary Officer Andrew J DeValles **Date** 20170721 **Time** 07:11

Results DISMISSED

Continuance Length ______ **Continuance Date** ______ **Projected Date** ______

20181212 11:54

COMMONWEALTH OF MASSACHUSETTS
DEPARTMENT OF CORRECTION
DISCIPLINARY REPORT

Inmate MCNEIL, DAVON **Commit No** W82395 **Location** RU (RECOVERY UNIT)

Date 20170720 **D- Report No** 392440 **Institution** OLD COLONY CORRECTIONAL CENTER

Reviewing Authority ______ **Date** ______ **Time** ______

20181212 11:54

Choices
Program Proposal
January 31, 2016

Cadre, Davon McNeil
Cadre, Jason Kwolek

9

CHAPTER NINE

CHOICES

Introduction

"Choices" was founded by me, Davon McNeil, and Jason Kwolek. This program is designed to impact the decision-making of today's youth in a positive and realistic way. We aim to make the youth deliberately aware of the tremendous negative effects of violence, drunk driving, drug dealing and drug usage; how they all have a ripple effect on families and communities. We want the youth to know that they will face many difficulties in their lives, but they don't have to face them alone. Parents, teachers, coaches and guidance counselors are there for them even when they (youth) think they're not. When the youth utter naive statements such as, "I'll never get caught," or "That won't happen to me," they're already making a poor decision. We will give them real-life examples of how we made poor decisions. We will provide an interactive awareness youth outreach program which attempts to show how poor decision-making can turn into the stark reality of prison life. The program will provide the youth with up-close-and- personal testimonies of incarcerated men who have made horrible choices in their lives and are reaping the consequences of their actions.

The following is a formal proposal for the formulation and implementation of the Choices program at Bridgewater State Hospital (BSH) medium security facility in Bridgewater, Massachusetts.

NOTE: Although the Choices program was denied by Superintendent Veronica Madden on 8/9/15 and again by Superintendent Daniel Calis on 2/18/16, I will never give up in my determination to have the Choices program implemented at Bridgewater State Hospital where I am a Cadre Inmate Worker.

Vision

We, as anti-crime and pro-life conscious people, can restore and bring clear mental thinking into the psyche of middle school, high school, college and at-risk youth organizations. We want to provide the youth with some real life tools that they can implement and use in their daily activities. This program will give youths the opportunity to experience making healthy choices which will in turn create healthy circumstances for themselves, ultimately leading to shaping a stable and pro-social environment for the betterment of society.

Mission

The mission of the Choices program is to impact the decision-making of today's youth in a positive and realistic way. We aim to make the youth deliberately aware of the tremendous negative effects of violence, drunk driving, drug dealing and drug usage; how it has a severe negative ripple effect on families and communities. We want the youth to know they will face many difficulties in their lives, but they don't have to face them alone. Parents, teachers, coaches and guidance counselors are there for them even when they (youth) think they're not. When the youth utter naive statements such as, "I'll never get caught," or "That won't happen to me," they're already making a poor decision. We will give them real-life examples of how we made poor decisions.

Curriculum

This curriculum is outlined with the objective of offering each youth the opportunity to: 1) participate in a question and answer segment with members of the Choices program where we will speak candidly about the consequences of positive/negative choices; 2) to foster self-worth and build confidence in the youth to combat peer pressure; and 3) to expose the youth to life changing tools and how to implement positive decision-making.

Process

Over the course of the school year we will schedule and meet with various schools and community youth organizations. The Choices program facilitators will take the initiative to reach out to prospective schools and youth groups via mailings (pamphlets) and community contacts. All responses and further communications will go through a BSH staff member. Scheduling will be based upon institutional/school availability.

This Choices program was developed as a volunteer give-back program to the youths of the community. Therefore this program will not offer "good time" or certificates. The two facilitators, in conjunction with the BSH staff, will select four cadres to participate in the Choices program for a total of six members.

Program Facilitators

The two Choices facilitators will be responsible for scheduling and preparing group members for events. They will host weekly meetings to develop, review or change program layouts as well as help with group member speech preparation. They will also be responsible for maintaining a written record of all program participant names, topics discussed and the agenda for the following week. All records will be available for review by the BSH staff.

Operational Requirements

Operational requirements for the Choices program, i.e. copies, pens and pads, will be provided by BSH staff. BSH staff will have final approval of all materials used.

Meeting Space

The Choices program events will be held within the visiting room to meet security guidelines. The weekly meetings will be held within a classroom or any space for program members to discuss the progress of the Choices program. The Choices program events will be held from 8:30 a.m. to 10:45 a.m. to avoid interruption of major count.

Scheduling

Scheduling will be based upon BSH staff and school/youth organization availability. Facilitators will manage the scheduling calendar and all pertinent information under direction of the BSH staff.

Summary

As I conclude, I will assure you that we will remain optimistic and fully committed to this joint endeavor. Our goal is to change the lives of youths by utilizing our own personal experiences and past mistakes to bring awareness to the types of choices they make every day. The key facilitators have developed a working relationship by consistently coming together in dialogue regarding our past choices and extreme diverse cultures. The proposal for the Choices youth outreach program is now officially submitted for your review and approval.

Respectfully,

Davon McNeil & Jason Kwolek

Me, in front of my Grandmother's House.

Me, at Souza Baranowski State Prison (The Max).

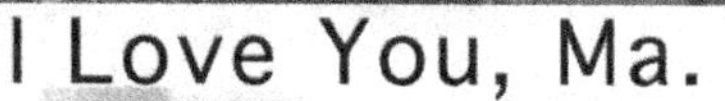

I Love You, Ma.

In Loving Memory of

Barbara M. McNeil

June 30, 1961
July 31, 2016

I'm Free

Don't grieve for me, for now I'm free,
I'm following the path God laid for me.
I took His hand when I heard Him call.
I turned my back and left it all.
I could not stay another day,
to laugh, to love, to work or play;
Tasks left undone must stay that way.
If my parting has left a void,
Then fill it with remembered joy.
A friendship shared, a laugh, a kiss,
Ah yes, these things too I will miss.
Be not burdened with times of sorrow,
I wish you the sunshine of tomorrow.
My life's been full, I've savored much.
Good friends, good times,
a loved ones touch.
Perhaps my time seemed all too brief,
Don't legthen it now with undue grief.
Lift up your hearts and share with me,
I'm with God now, I've been set free.

Funerarias Multi Culturel Brockton, MA

Me & my man, Joey.

Me, at my graduation (G.E.D.); At Bridgewater State Hospital (Cadre Program).

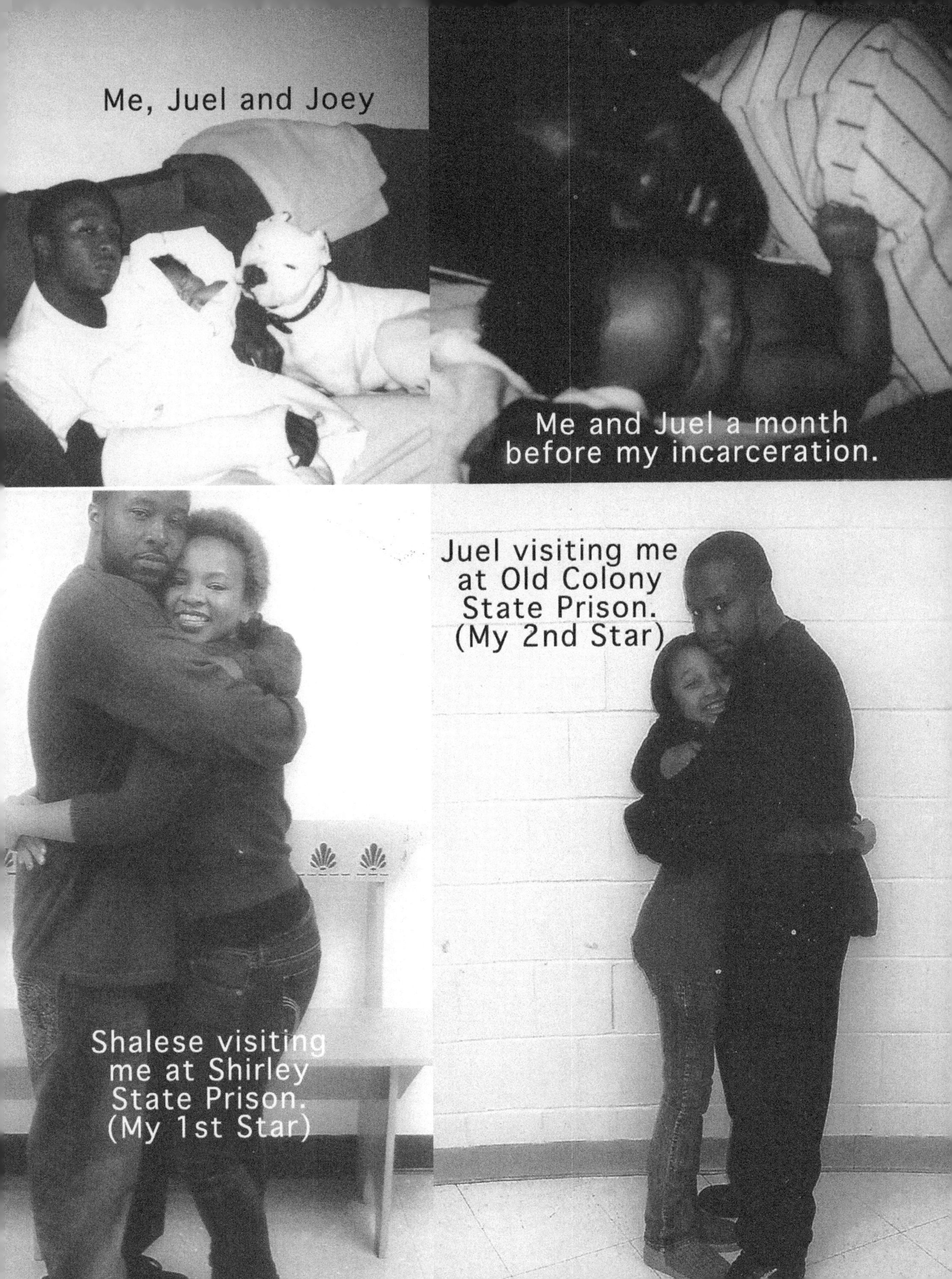

Me, Juel and Joey

Me and Juel a month before my incarceration.

Shalese visiting me at Shirley State Prison. (My 1st Star)

Juel visiting me at Old Colony State Prison. (My 2nd Star)

PART FOUR

The Journey

10

CHAPTER TEN

MY STORY

On July 24, 2000, my grandmother's front door was kicked in by the Boston Violent Youth Task Force and Brockton homicide detectives. I was arrested and charged with 1st degree murder. I was twenty-two years old. I was transported to the Brockton police station where I was searched, booked on 1st degree murder chargers and fingerprinted; had my picture taken numerous times; allowed to make my one phone call; and promptly placed in a holding cell.

Then the following morning I was transported to Brockton District Court and arraigned on 1st degree murder charges. The judge set my bail at one million dollars. And after my arraignment I was transported to the Plymouth House of Corrections where I awaited trial for approximately three years and four months.

On September 15, 2003, I was tried and convicted in Brockton Superior Court by a jury of five men and seven women. The judge (Richard J. Chin) sentenced me to 15 years to life. I had many supporters during my trial which lasted for one and a half weeks. There were many things which occurred in my trial that I didn't agree with and found to be extremely unfair. But I've come to the realization, through maturity, that none of those things would have happened if I hadn't chosen to walk down that crooked path, living a life of crime which ultimately led me to taking a young man's life.

I arrived at MCI Concord (State Prison) on September 15, 2003 at 5:45 p.m. I was tired, stressed, angry and afraid, and I honestly didn't know what to expect. I went through a rigorous intake process where my picture was taken at least 20 times and finger-printed continuously. I filled out ten different questionnaires and I answered a ton of questions asked by officers, doctors and mental health workers. I was allowed to make one phone call so I decided to call my grandmother's house because I knew all my family members would be there after leaving the courthouse.

My father answered the phone and as soon as he heard my voice, he broke down in tears. After pulling himself together he explained to me that he felt responsible for my situation. He told me that he loved me with all his heart and that he was sorry for not being there for me while I was growing up. He said that I had a long road ahead of me and there were two ways that I could do my time in prison: I could either continue down the negative path which would only get tougher, or I could utilize my time to change my life for the better. But it was a choice only I could make.

My grandmother could hardly speak due to her continuous crying, but she managed to collect herself after I assured her that I was alright. She told me that she loved me very much and always tried to raise me right. She begged me to stay strong and not to get myself into any trouble. She said she would come to visit me as soon as possible and would send me some money. She kept repeating how much she loved me through her tears.

It was really hard for me to speak to my mother. In that very moment, it felt as though I'd done nothing except cause her a great amount of heartache and pain. And here she was, crying again because of me. Through my own tears I told her that I was sorry for all that I had put her through. I did my best to explain to her that it wasn't her fault. I chose to live my life in the streets and commit crimes. I told her she did the best that she could as a single mother raising three boys on her own; I told her she was my number one lady and I loved her so much. I could mentally see her smiling on the other end of the phone. She didn't say too much to me during the phone call because she was heartbroken by my conviction. She'd fainted in the courtroom when the judge sentenced me.

My auntie (Debbie) was next. She said she wasn't going to cry like everyone else. She got straight to the point by saying, "Hootie (the name she called me), you already know what time it is. You chose to play in the streets and now you're paying for playing!" She told me to keep my head up and stay out of trouble. She said she would send me some money by the next day and come visit me the following week. Then she told me she loved me and passed the phone to my aunt-mom, Meta.

My aunt-mom and I share a very special bond. I have never called her "auntie" a day in my life. I've called her "ma" ever since I learned to talk. She instantly got on the phone and started cussing out the judge and district attorney. She felt as though they were working together in a conspiracy along with my lawyer. But she eventually calmed down and told me how much she loved me. She told me she'd come and visit me in a few days. She assured me that no matter what, she and my family would be by my side every step of the way.

It felt really good speaking to my family and hearing their loving words of support. But after the phone call ended, reality began to sink in. I was in a State prison, about to experience things that the outside world couldn't fathom. But what I didn't know was that I was also about to meet men who would share priceless words of wisdom with me who would die in prison many years later. Life as I understood it in that moment would become obsolete.

In prison word travels fast. By the time I entered new man (units men/women are housed in when they first enter prison), inmates I didn't even know approached me with messages directing me to go to the prison yard at the next movement (recreation period). Now, I didn't know if I was being summoned to the prison yard by a friend or an enemy; but it really didn't matter because either way I was going. However, on my way there I was filled with many different emotions because I had no idea what I was walking into. And entering the yard was like a high school flashback. I was shocked at the number of persons waiting for me. Some I went to high school with and hadn't seen them in years. So, while walking around a running track, they took turns enlightening me about the rules of prison. Most of the rules didn't make sense to me at all. There were so many it began to make me dizzy trying to remember them all. But I figured these guys knew better than me, so I listened intently to what was being said.

The next six months passed by in a blur as we walked the yard, reminiscing about our past lives in the streets. Most of us were doing serious time in prison so we escaped that harsh reality by staying stuck in memories of our pasts. Unbeknownst to me, I was about to be transferred to one of the most violent institutions in Massachusetts (Souza Baranowski aka The Max) where there would be no escaping the reality of prison life at all.

My first day in new man in The Max I witnessed a young Puerto Rican get his face sliced open with a prison-made knife. He was an active gang member who ran into a rival gang member. I was instructed by an elder prisoner who knew my father from his many years in prison, to never leave my cell without my sneakers on my feet; no matter what. As I observed my surroundings I noticed that every prisoner went into the shower stalls wearing their sneakers. The shower door locked us inside and once we heard the click of the lock, we'd remove our sneakers. Gang members would stand guard outside the shower stall while their comrades showered safely.

Souza Baranowski prison was and is a training ground for anti-social, paranoid schizophrenic, hyper-sensitive and egotistical personality destroyers. Almost every young prisoner there was extremely angry and looking to build a reputation by committing violent acts.

But I've also met some of the most intelligent men of wisdom during my stay behind the walls of The Max. Old Man Smitty (Hubert Smith) had been incarcerated for thirty-one years at the time of our introduction. He took a liking to me because of my consistent workout regimen and the fact that I wasn't a follower. He was fifty-nine years old with a body sculpted like a GI Joe action figure (seriously). We would silently watch each other while doing our calisthenics in the prison yard.

One day it was pouring rain in the yard and only 10 to 15 guys were willing to brave the soaking. I was completing my seventh set of pull-ups when Old Man Smitty approached me and asked, "Hey young brother. How many sets are you doing?"

"I'm doing twenty sets," I answered.

"Do you mind if I jump in with you?" he asked.

With an arrogant and cocky smile, I responded, "Let's get it, Old Head!"

That workout was the start of a friendship which has lasted to this very day. And I have to admit that he worked me into the ground during many of our intense workout sessions in the prison yard. Smitty is serving a natural life prison sentence. He has come to terms with the devastating reality that he may one day die in its catacomb. We've shared some very deep conversations regarding the true meaning of life and how decades spent in physical confinement can destroy a man's psyche.

I will forever treasure and remember Smitty's lesson on Cognitive Dissonance. We were sitting in his cell, drinking green tea with honey, and he began to explain to me that our attitudes can affect our behavior and our behavior can affect our attitude. This information was 100% foreign to me. But I listened because Smitty was very serious about educating the young men in prison. He explained that the Cognitive Dissonance theory proves that when our beliefs and attitudes oppose each other, or our behavior, we are motivated to reduce the dissonance through changes in our behavior or cognition (perception). He said that the theory itself has been influential in predicting behavior that reflects an inconsistency in attitudes. He also explained that most men in prison who decide to change their lives for the better experience cognitive dissonance. He told me that positive/negative thoughts cannot coexist, therefore behaving in such a way which conflicts with their attitude. This causes pressure to change the attitude in order to be consistent with their behavior. I would come to completely understand his lesson years later when I would experience cognitive dissonance in a real way.

In 2006, I was housed in Unit P-2 (in The Max) when I made a collect phone call to my mother. My little brother, Booda, answered and informed me our mother was in the hospital having surgery to amputate her right leg due to complications from diabetes. He also told me my mother had become addicted to heroin and wasn't in good health. And in addition, his next words were almost too much to bear: my baby brother, Andre, had been shot two weeks earlier.

In the following weeks after I learned about the situations at home, I experienced a great deal of depression. But I was ignorant to the symptoms of depression at that time. Today, I'm cognizant of the fact that the majority of men in prison suffer from the effects of depression. We've all suffered sadness and we've all been in a bad mood. However, when we say "I'm depressed" today, it's not the proper description for our suffering. Depression—technically called clinical or major depression—is not a twenty-four hour bug. It's a serious mood disorder in which there are severe changes in a person's behavior, emotions, cognition and physical functions.

A diagnosis of depression must include an overwhelming feeling of sadness and/or worthlessness which must last at least two or more weeks and disrupt your daily life. The symptoms of depression also include a lack of desire to do anything, even things you loved to do in the past; thoughts of death and suicide; a lack of energy; a change in appetite (over eating or not eating); changes in sleeping patterns (inability to fall asleep or sleeping a lot more than usual); difficulty concentrating and making decisions; and a lack of desire to be social. I experienced all these symptoms after that phone conversation with my brother, Booda.

The only way I was able to maintain my sanity through this turbulent time was by painting mental pictures of the life I would create for myself upon my release from prison. Drawing these pictures within my mind allowed me to develop a degree of hope. They were pictures of me spending quality time with my family and my two beautiful daughters. Also, I read an assortment of books dealing with self-help methods, black history and various breeds of dogs to keep me distracted. This was an extremely trying period of time for me because I felt hopeless, as if I had no control over my life.

During this crucible, Souza Baranowski was furnished with single cells throughout the entire facility. I awoke in my cell one night at approximately 3:00 a.m. in a cold sweat with a heavy heart. I couldn't figure out what was going on with me. As I lay still on my bunk, in complete darkness, my two daughters' faces kept flashing though my subconscious. Restless, I got up and turned the light on in the cell. I opened the photo album which contained pictures of my daughters and slowly began to turn each page while staring at the reflections of my babies. I felt my chest tighten and my breathing became laborious. It seemed as if though my daughters were talking to me through the pictures, asking me, "Daddy, why did you leave us in the world by ourselves without your guidance and protection?" I closed the album and walked over to the mirror. As I stood there staring at my reflection, I asked myself over and over, "Davon, what have you done?" Suddenly, I began crying uncontrollably. I didn't realize it in that moment but my conscience was being awakened. My life prior to incarceration caused me to unconsciously bury my conscience (a knowledge or feeling of right and wrong; moral judgment). I suffered tremendously from a severe case of apathy (a lack of emotions; indifference). There are a number of causatives to the above effects, but not having a self-identity was the root cause.

The following day I asked Smitty to meet with me in the prison library. In vivid detail I explained to him what I had experienced. His face lit up with a huge smile. He said, "Brother, the God within you is striving to get your attention. You've been anchored by your past for so long that you're emotionally frozen into your childhood suffering. You've got to let go of that deep-rooted anger that's holding you hostage because it's blinding your inner vision. The wounded and hurt inner child you were forced to bury is now reaching out to you for a hug."

The divine wisdom which Smitty was bestowing upon me didn't make any sense to me. But out of my respect for him, I sat there and listened. He continued. "Brother, not too many young men are blessed with your experience. That was divine intervention. You're being called to do something great with your life. But if you don't take heed and answer the call by tapping into your divinity, you're going to be chastised with a severe punishment. I see how you carry yourself and you've got a good head on your shoulders. Please don't miss your calling, young brother!"

The next few days were like walking in the desert. I was desperately searching for knowledge (information) to help me understand what I was going through. I honestly didn't know where to start. Then one day I was at my job detail which was me basically cleaning the school building. As I was sweeping the hallway floor, Clair—who was the GED teacher—called me into her empty classroom.

"Mr. McNeil, do you have your GED?" she asked me.

"No," I answered.

"Well, why not?"

"Mrs. Clair, I've got plenty of time left on my sentence to get my GED. And besides. I'm not focused right now and my mind is all over the place," I replied.

"Mr. McNeil, do you mind if I ask you what you're focused on, and why do you think your mind is scattered?"

"I honestly don't know," I responded. I told her it felt as if though my life was at a standstill. I revealed to her some of the things I had experienced in the past few weeks.

She listened to me without saying a word. We shared a short period of silence and then she said,

"Mr. McNeil, it sounds as if you're internally conflicted."

The look on my face expressed I had no clue as to what she was talking about.

"Mr. McNeil, being in prison is very unnatural. It causes a person to experience many different conflicting emotions. And when you do not have the proper tools to deal with these emotions the effects can be everlasting. When we cannot have the best of both worlds such as needing money to buy a car while needing the car to get to the job which supplies you with money, a conflict of emotions/motives occurs. This is something I personally experienced, Mr. McNeil. And finding a working solution to this conflict produced a lot of stress for me, especially when help from my family and friends was unavailable. Therefore, I can honestly relate to some of the emotions you're feeling. But I will never say I fully understand what you go through on a day-to-day basis living in prison. From what I gather, you realize that you've done something terribly wrong which caused you to leave your daughters without a father. And knowing there is nothing you can do about it is causing you a great deal of conflicting emotions.

Mr. McNeil, conflict manifests itself in many forms. And most young men in prison lack a basic understanding of how to recognize these conflicts taking place within them. It is not in the DOC's best interest to provide you young men with this information and it sickens me because they know exactly what the remedy is; but there's no profit in fixing the problem. I talk to young men everyday who suffer from many of its effects and I strive to make it my business to enlighten you guys to the best of my ability," she said.

"Now, Mr. McNeil, let me tell you how stress affects mental health," Mrs. Clair said to me. "You're not alone in your struggle! But you have to study, study, study. Listen carefully. Along with physical illness, psychological reactions to stressful events can hinder our ability to think clearly and logically. In a panic, a person might be so caught up in worrying about the repercussions of a negative end-result that they fail to take the proper steps needed to cause a positive end-result. For example, a person starts firing a gun in a crowded nightclub filled with hundreds of people. Everyone's initial panicked response is to run for the exits. Some people can be trampled or crushed in the process. Some people worry so much about the possible consequences of a decision that they can't make the correct decision. Therefore, the wrong decision gets made for them," she said, looking at me to see if I understood.

"This information is very important for you to understand and research yourself. Your wellbeing and mental harmony depends on it. Mr. McNeil, what is your definition of anxiety, anger and depression? What do these three things mean to you?"

My answer to Mrs. Clair's question must have made her very uncomfortable because her face became flushed. Then she began to educate me. She told me the following:

Anxiety: the tense feeling you get when you are worried about bad things that might happen in the future. Anxiety is categorized into two types: objective anxiety and neurotic anxiety.

Objective anxiety is described as a person's realistic approach to the situation causing the anxiety. The person is prompted to act in order to get rid of the anxiety they're feeling. Neurotic anxiety is anxiety which is believed to be caused by unconscious driven intentions which the person does not recognize; therefore, is unable to understand or control.

Anger: a response to stress which often produces some form of aggressive behavior. The frustration/aggression hypothesis presumes that when our attempts are hindered when trying to get what we want, we become frustrated; an emotion which causes us to act aggressively by trying to injure the person or thing which is causing the frustration. A bad day at work might take the form of a verbal argument with a family member. And problems in a marriage may emerge as unusual behavior in social situations.

Depression: when all sense of hope is lost and the desire to live a full, healthy, goal-oriented life has diminished. Depression takes over every aspect of a person's being, including disrupting their eating and sleeping habits, their thought processes and the ability to form and sustain positive relationships. While signs of depression can be identified, what leads to depression and who is more apt to become depressed is yet to be determined. A combination of events as well as a single experience can trigger depression; and all personality types are susceptible.

I was taking in everything she was telling me and finally she said, "Mr. McNeil, you can take this worksheet with you but please make sure you study it, alright? If you come back tomorrow I'll have a few more worksheets, and maybe a book for you to read. I know this information is all new to you, but if you're serious about healing yourself, you'll need to do some intense studying and research. Do you own a dictionary?"

"No ma'am," I responded.

"Well, take one off that shelf. You can keep it. Also, I'm adding your name to my list of potential GED students, too!"

I left Mrs. Clair's classroom feeling good; as if a burden had been lifted off my shoulders. But I never made it back to see Mrs. Clair because I was transferred from Souza Baranowski to Old Colony Correctional Center the very next day. I had been confined within the walls of a maximum security prison for two and a half years. It was time to continue on my journey. But, I had no idea what awaited me.

My arrival at Old Colony Correctional Center was a breath of fresh air. The tension in the atmosphere was miniscule in comparison to The Max. I wasn't mentally prepared to deal with the high degree of unrestricted movement throughout this new environment. As word spread around the prison of my arrival, many of the men came to greet me in new man. Once again, guys I hadn't seen in twenty years were now standing before me with huge smiles plastered on their faces. These guys made sure I had the basic necessities and gave me a brief, verbal rundown of the prison operations.

At breakfast the next morning I was approached by someone claiming to be Bruce Montrond's (the victim in my case) cousin. He said that he and I had to lock in (fight) because I was responsible for killing his cousin. We agreed to meet in the prison yard during the 9:00 a.m. movement. I had been incarcerated for seven years without any problems or physical altercations. But in the back of my mind I always knew I'd have to reap what I had sown. That day had finally arrived. I honestly didn't want to fight this guy and risk losing my chance of being granted a positive parole decision at my upcoming parole hearing. But I knew that I couldn't back down because my reputation was on the line. And as he'd said, I was responsible for his cousin's death. Therefore, I knew he wasn't going to let me back down even if I wanted to, so to the yard I went.

However, unbeknownst to me, Millie (the guy who wanted to fight me) was doing a 15 to life prison sentence like me. He also had a parole hearing coming up and was actually good friends with one of the guys who came to greet me while I was in new man. This guy, Tony, and I had gone to high school together. So when he got the word about my upcoming fight in the yard he quickly mediated the potential chaos. When Millie showed up in the yard wanting to talk instead of fight, I was extremely happy. We walked around the yard and spoke like two, civilized grown men. We both came to the realization we made terrible mistakes in our pasts and wanted to use our time in prison to become better men. We both had daughters whom we loved very much and wanted to get home to them as soon as possible. This cathartic experience would benefit me in a big way many years later.

In mid-2007 a key witness who testified against me at my trial signed an affidavit admitting that he lied at my trial by giving false testimony. Based on the signed affidavit, I was granted an evidentiary hearing. It's rare that a prisoner is granted this type of hearing once he has been convicted in a court of law. As a result, I was overjoyed and in high spirits with this new turn of events.

I needed some assistance with my legal situation and upcoming hearing. After asking for help from a few guys who were considered to be good jailhouse lawyers, I was guided by word- of-mouth to a person who called himself Allah Fu-Quan. He was rumored to be highly proficient in the language of the law. So Allah Fu-Quan and I met up in the prison library to discuss my legal issues.

"Peace black man. My name is Allah Fu-Quan. How can I be of service to you?"

"What's up? My name is Davon but everyone calls me Vee. I want to know how much you'll charge me to help me with my legal issues. I've been granted an evidentiary hearing by the courts and I need some assistance with preparing my case for the upcoming hearing."

"Black Man I'm not the 10% (anyone who knows the truth and charges to share it with others). I'm not going to charge you any gold (money) to help you potentially obtain your physical freedom. It's my duty and responsibility to show you my highest equality."

At that first meeting with Allah Fu-Quan I honestly thought he was crazy. And I didn't understand all those big words he was using. But he was rumored to be a genius with the law so I stuck around. Unfortunately, the legal assistance I received from Allah Fu-Quan didn't help me achieve my physical freedom. Instead, he helped me in a way which was priceless. Fu-Quan helped me to discover my true self! Through the guidance and patience given to me by Allah Fu-Quan, I was able to gain Supreme Mental Freedom.

It was during my third meeting with him in the law library when I decided to ask him if he was some type of Muslim or something. I had never in my life heard, nor seen anyone speak, or carry themselves in such a refined and disciplined manner. He denied being a Muslim and explained to me that Muslims are those who submit themselves to the will of Allah and believe in a mystery heaven above the clouds. Allah Fu-Quan told me that he was God-Centered and submitted only to His supreme thoughts. He said heaven and hell were only mental conditions which we create for ourselves based upon our way of thinking and living. Our way of thinking manifests our reality here on earth. I went back to my cell, laid down and meditated on what Fu-Quan had said to me.

As time passed I found myself spending a lot of time in the company of this wise young man. I learned that he was sentenced to natural life in prison. But his ways and actions never reflected such a harsh reality.

One hot summer's day we were casually walking in the yard, he looked into my eyes and asked me one of the most important questions of my life.

"Vee, who are you?" he asked.

I didn't give his question any real thought before I began to spew out a bunch of nonsense about how loyal I am; how I'm well respected in the streets; and how much I live my life by the unwritten rules of the underworld (streets). In mid-sentence Fu-Quan cut me off.

"Black Man, I don't want to hear about who you think you are according to the dead world (the streets)," he said. "I want to know who you are within your internal self. Who are YOU?"

I instantly became frustrated. I felt myself becoming mad at him. Who the fuck did he think he was to question me about who I am? Was this dude trying to disrespect me? Was he trying to belittle me? These were questions I silently asked myself as we quietly walked the prison yard. Allah Fu-Quan must have picked up on my negative vibrations/energy. He stopped walking, turned to look at me and said, "Black Man, do not speak to me again until you can tell me exactly who you are!" Then he walked away from me and left me standing in the middle of the yard.

I was livid! I returned to my cell, feeling completed humiliated, angry and confused. I paced the small 8'xlO' confined space, asking myself over and over, "Davon, who are you?"

For the second time during my seven years of incarceration I broke down and cried. I honestly had no idea who I was. Damn, who was I? Why didn't I know who I was?

I dodged Fu-Quan for as long as I could. Then one day he cornered me in the chow hall (cafeteria). He said, "Peace, Black Man, are you striving to avoid me?"

"I avoid no man!" I responded.

He smiled at me and asked me to meet him in the library at the 1:00 p.m. movement. When we met he said, "Black Man, the reason that you don't know who you are is because your true identity has been stolen from you. From birth you've been fed the wrong food, both mentally and physically. You're the Asiatic Black Man. You're the maker and owner of the planet earth. You're the father of civilization and God of the universe. You were birthed out of your mother's womb as the sole controller and original author of your own destiny. But the true knowledge of yourself has been diabolically stripped away from you. Therefore, a lack of knowledge has kept you bound to a triple stage of 100% mental darkness. Brother, do you think that you're in prison by choice? Do you think that you consciously chose to wake up one morning and say to yourself, "Hmmm, I think I'll go to prison today? Black Man, you're great! But you have to realize your greatness is buried deep within you. Start the process of unearthing it!"

For the next three days my head was spinning from the divine wisdom I received from Fu-Quan. I learned that he was a sincere adherent of the Nation of Gods and Earths. This is a nation of black men, women and children—and a small percentage of Caucasians—dedicated to bringing awareness to the lost people here in the wilderness of North America. Also, I learned that the Nations of Gods and Earths do not consider themselves Muslims and were emphatic about showing and proving that they were not a gang. Their basic foundational teaching is that they're not pro-black or anti-white. They teach that they are anti-devilishment and pro- righteous! These righteous men, women and children are totally against drug usage, violence, selling of drugs, guns, gang culture, racism, etc. They're a God-Centered Nation and live their lives based upon the principles of Supreme Mathematics and Supreme Alphabets. The Supreme Mathematics consist of ten numerical principles; the Supreme Alphabets consist of the twenty- six letters of the alphabets broken down into words with divine meaning to each word. I was amazed that the teachings of the Nation of Gods and Earths had attracted hardcore criminals and turned these men and women into civilized and law-abiding citizens. Fu-Quan explained to me that everything in the universe was governed by mathematics. And these were ancient teachings which were lost to the original people of the planet earth.

One morning I woke up feeling real low on energy. The feeling lasted all day. I called my girlfriend around 7:30 p.m. and as soon as she heard my voice she asked, "Davon, what's wrong? Are you alright?" I explained to her that it was nothing major and that I was a little mentally stressed and feeling down. I expressed to her that I was tired of being in prison and wanted to come home to be with her, our daughter and my family. I told her I wanted to change my life for the better; I wanted to be a good husband and father. She advised me to remain strong and told me that she'd come to visit me in a few days. We said "I love you" to each other and ended the call.

Later that night I was locked in my cell and decided to read a few pages of the Bible. I turned to a passage in the book of Psalm (verse 82:6) which states, "Ye are all gods and children of the Most High God." I placed the Bible on the steel writing table and lay down on the bed. I began to take a serious look at myself and the life I led before my incarceration. I really wanted to change my life for the better but I just didn't know where, or how, to start. Then suddenly, it slapped me in my face like a ton of bricks. I thought I was going crazy when I thought I heard Old Man Smitty whispering to me. I got out of bed quickly, clicked the light switch on and stared at myself in the mirror. Davon, are you losing your damn mind? Then Smitty's voice got louder. "Brother, in a state of cognitive dissonance people may sometimes feel disequilibrium, frustration, dread, quilt, anger, embarrassment, anxiety, etc. This is normal and necessary before any mental resurrection can take place. " My entire body began to feel light. I was filled with an overwhelming degree of calmness. I couldn't stop smiling as I continued to gaze at my reflection in the mirror. I was about to take my life into my own hands and change for the better because I was worth it!

As soon as the doors of the cells were opened for breakfast I made a mad dash in search of Allah Fu-Quan. He was sitting with a group of his brothers from the Nation of Gods and Earths when I approached their table, out of breath, from a mixture of excitement and my sprint to the chow hall (cafeteria). It was 7:30 in the morning and I looked Allah Fu-Quan in the eyes and said, "Peace,

Black Man. I'm ready to swim my 9,000 miles back home (change my life)."

I will forever remember the smile on his face as he told me to meet him in the yard at the 1:00 p.m. movement.

In the middle of the baseball field, Fu-Quan asked me, "'Why do you want to change your life?"

"I'm tired of going through hell!" I responded. "You told me that hell is a mental condition that we create for ourselves by the thoughts we manifest. I've been creating hell for myself and loved ones for a long time. Now, it's time for me to change my life. I feel as if though this prison shit is killing me, Fu. My mother is in the world sick and suffering from heroin addiction. And my two daughters are being raised without their father, all because I chose to live a lifestyle that was designed for me to fail."

"Black Man, I'm willing to invest my time in order to help you see the true reality of exactly who and what you are. But I need you to firmly understand that this journey is long, lonely, and hard. It takes full discipline for you to sincerely change and deal with the atoning element. Brother, forgiving yourself is the very first step and it's not going to happen overnight. The true nature of the original man (Black Man) is holy and divine. Within you is the Kingdom of God. Your body is the temple of God. And as God, you must live and move as such. You need not seek in the sky or in your imagination for anything or anyone greater than yourself. In order to find Allah (God) incarnate, you must start looking within his home, his temple, his being; it's in you.

Brother, God means Supreme Being. And Supreme means Most High. Being is an existing person (male and female). This means we have to be responsible and accountable for our words and actions. If we can do that, we will become Supreme in knowledge, wisdom, understanding and power. A being has a form, mass and structure. Therefore God has a body! That which has a body is made of bones, flesh and blood. I will help you, Brother. But first, you've got to help yourself by being 100% serious about your growth and development."

I explained to Fu-Quan that I take my life seriously and I fully understood the wisdom he was sharing with me. I thanked him for taking the time to help me and told him I would not let him, or myself, down. I was completely dissatisfied with the wild illusion I was living. After spending seven years of my life in prison, I came to realize the way of life we call "The Game" is truly not a game at all. I was led to believe that I could have all that which my heart desired as long as I stayed loyal to the code of the streets. But in reality I only experienced hard times, death, destruction, pain, heartache and a 15-to-life prison sentence.

All of my so-called friends disappeared when I came to prison. I gave my all to the streets and she (the streets) gave me her ass to kiss. I spent many long days and nights trapped in those hallways and standing on street comers selling poison (drugs) which destroyed my community. I cannot tell you how much flesh I lost from being chased by the police. I've had my lungs collapse on me as well as broken bones in my body. And, I'd also been shot. All because I made the streets my first love! It was definitely time for me to change my life because I refused to allow that negative lifestyle to hold me within its foul embrace. I had been shut up in my own mental darkness for too many years. Then a strategy began to take shape in my mind.

I decided to spend two hours a day with Allah Fu-Quan, allowing him to teach me whatever he felt I needed to know at this stage in my journey. Also, I would do independent studying in my cell. I wanted to honestly find out why I thought the way I did prior to incarceration. I wanted to fully comprehend why my life turned out the way it did. However, the scariest part was when I would sit quietly with my own thoughts. After existing in such a lost state of mind for so long, the idea of developing a conscience to counter the injustice of my own ignorance, terrified me. When I was ignorant and living my life as a savage in the pursuit of happiness, I didn't have to be responsible or accountable for my actions. Well, at least that's what I thought!

During one of my sessions with Fu, he explained that it was a prerequisite that I participate in a 3-day fast (abstaining from all solid food) as a means to purify my body and develop an extraordinary degree of discipline for my internal self. He told me that learning to fast would create self-control and a willingness to sacrifice for the achievement of goals. In that moment I knew for sure Allah Fu-Quan was a complete lunatic. How would I survive not eating for three straight days? I was convinced I'd die! But he assured me I would be alright. Plus, he assured me he would fast with me. But I still wasn't too sure about not eating for three days. As I reflect back on the experience of fasting for three days, it makes me smile.

I learned that nothing and no one was going to do the work for me. I'd have to go through many difficult emotions that accompanied change, growth and development. A part of my regimen was to sit in the center of my cell floor for one hour every day, seven days a week, in complete silence. I was striving to quiet the noise within my mind so I could hear my thoughts clearly. That was one of the hardest of my tasks. The mind is a powerful tool and if not controlled or utilized correctly, it can cause great harm to your existence. Therefore, I was fully committed to mastering my thoughts. I cannot put into words how it made me feel when I was defeated by my thoughts. Your worst enemy cannot hurt you as much as your own thoughts when you haven't mastered them.

As time passed, I was able to center myself and conquer the negative voice in my head. Our perception is extremely important for our wellbeing; for our serenity and mental peace. It (perception) should be free from negative emotions and ignorance as well as free from illusions. Slowly, I began to feel better about myself and was able to slowly move into the next phase of my self-taught program. This phase consisted of forgiving "me" for all the wrong I'd done.

The program I created was paying off tremendously. I discovered how to love and accept myself for who I was: the good, the bad and the ugly. I learned that in its simplest form, self- acceptance means accepting yourself fully for the person you are regardless to whom or what. Self-acceptance comes from an acceptance of the things you like about yourself and the things you cannot change about yourself. Learning to accept my flaws was a process which involved a willingness to experience thoughts, feelings and emotions without denial. I didn't have to like everything I accepted. I simply had to learn that reality is reality, and running away from my reality wouldn't solve my problems.

My grandmother came to visit me and it was one of my happiest days in prison. During my first few years of incarceration I learned a prisoner should never get dressed for a visit until the officer calls out their name. I've sat in my cell, fully dressed, on many occasions only to have my supposed visitor never show up. But this time I was fully dressed when the officer called my name. When my grandma tells me she is coming to visit me, you can bet your last dollar that she's coming to see her Peter Pan (a name that only she calls me).

I walked into the visiting room and seeing my grandma waiting for me brought a huge smile to my face. But I also experienced some pain. She looked so small and frail and had lost a lot of weight since I last saw her. I looked into her eyes which told me she was sick. When she stood up to hug me, I ran into her loving arms and warm embrace. Hugging her instantly brought back memories from my childhood. We both cried in each other's arms. As we took our seats my grandmother sat there in silence, staring at my face with a beautiful smile etched on her face. I emulated her smile until my face began to hurt.

"I love you, Peter Pan!" she said.

"I love you more, grandma," I replied.

"Baby, how are you doing?" she asked.

"I responded by saying, "I'm doing wonderful! Look at me! I'm young, black and extremely handsome." I always knew exactly what to say to put a smile on my grandmother's face. My response worked like a charm.

"Peter Pan, are you keeping warm in this place? Do you have thermals to wear? Are these people feeding you good in here? Do you have all of your toiletries?" she asked.

"I'm fine," I replied. "I have everything I need. Grandma, enough about me. How are you doing?"

"Baby, that's one of the reasons I've come to visit you. Your grandma hasn't been feeling too good these days." As soon as she uttered those words I instantly began to cry. "No, you wipe away them tears. You hear me, son? I didn't come all the way up here to watch you cry. Son, you listen and you listen good, you hear?" I nodded my head as tears dripped down my face. She continued. "I did my best to raise you right and with some sense. You are a good boy and don't ever let anyone convince you otherwise. But you were always a man-child and wanted to run in those filthy streets. Them streets have never meant you no good, baby. Peter Pan, I need for you to understand that grandma is sick. And I don't know how much longer the good Lord is going to keep me on this earth. I need you to promise me something, Peter Pan. I need you to promise your grandma that when you leave out of here (prison), you will not be the same as you came in. Baby, can you promise me that?"

I looked at my grandmother and said, "Grandma, I promise you I will not leave out of here the same as I came in! I promise you, grandma!" She didn't know that my transformation had already begun.

"Peter Pan, I'm not sure if I'll be around to see if you fulfill your promise to me, but I'll damn sure be watching you. You hear? Baby, no matter what them people in that courtroom said that you did, it's between you and God! But you have to repent and ask God for forgiveness. You've always been a loving and deeply caring child. You just grew-up too fast. And your aunts didn't help none with all that grass (marijuana) they smoked and cussing they was doing," she said with a smile. I had a wonderful visit with my grandmother.

My grandmother passed away a year later. I was devastated! The Department of Corrections denied my request to attend my grandmother's wake because according to them my grandmother was not my legal guardian. This was a real trying time for me because their decision made me hot with anger. How could they be so cruel and not allow me to see my grandmother for the very last time? I went into seclusion for approximately three weeks before I had a session with Fu-Quan and that's when he dropped a jewel on me.

"Peace, Black Man! You have to come to the divine realization that we're dealing with a nefarious natured people. Their entire system is based on separation and destruction. But we give them the power to keep us separated from our loved ones when we fall victim to their uncivilized ways (street life). Their cave-like mentality was created over 6,000 years ago; and they were made for a purpose. They only exist too cause chaos and confusion among the righteous and original people of the planet earth. By not allowing you free transportation to attend your grand old earth's (my grandmother) wake is a part of their trick knowledge. Their duty is to cause you to be other than your natural self — which is God Centered.

Black Man, you can never allow Satan to rule your best part (mind). You must remain perpendicular on your square of truth at all times. All you have to do is keep the memories of your grand old earth alive within your attic (mind). Your grand old earth will forever be a part of your physical composition because you're the son of her son. But most importantly, you have to fulfill your promise to her by transcending this ominous world. I know it hurts, but you're stronger mentally and physically than any weakness the devil strives to tempt you with. Peace is the way of the righteous!"

I decided to use my anger as fuel to propel me into a greater realm of growth and development. There was no way I was going to allow the denial to attend my grandmother's wake to defeat my progress. I had come too far in my recovery to let such an evil act take me off my righteous path. I figured that I could only beat the system by outgrowing it. If the system functions on chaos and confusion, I had to function on supreme law and order. I had to operate from a high degree of mental peace and harmony. I had to educate myself in the science of cause and effect. I had to get intimate with the root causes of anger. I had to study black history and learn about the struggles of all my ancestors who came before me. I will not allow the system to break me. I'm worth a better life!

On December 1, 2007, I committed myself to completely changing for the better. There would be no days off from the arduous task of recreating myself. I spent a week meeting up with various people who I knew from my past life in the streets as well as those I had formed bonds with in prison. I explained to each person that it was time for me to change my life for the better. I made it real clear that I didn't want any of them to think that my sudden change in attitude and behavior was anything personal towards them. I told them I was refraining from all negativity; I would not be coming to the prison yard to hang out; and I would no longer discuss anything regarding my past lifestyle, unless I was using it as a teaching opportunity for a younger prisoner. Surprisingly, I was greeted with a lot of respect and support from these individuals.

But I knew deep inside their minds they thought I was going through some kind of faze. In prison there's a huge stigma associated with a guy who decides to change his life for the better. Usually one of two things have occurred: He found God, or he has lost his mind!

All of the things I am doing today in my life were within the reach of my talents prior to my coming to prison sixteen years ago. But I did not see myself as capable back then. I had a limited vision of my own abilities and that restricted my growth. I was stuck in a mud hole of my own creation; trapped in a mental cage I had constructed for myself. I wasn't doing all that I could because I couldn't see beyond the wall of my limitations to the horizons of my infinite possibilities. But now, my passion has matured into seeking the greater good within all people. And I always have to be careful with expressing my passion with others, especially here in prison. Prison has stolen the souls of many great men.

In the tranquility of my internal world and the stillness of my mind, I can hear the souls of my fellow prisoners crying out for help. I'm able to look into their eyes and clearly see their tortured and pain-stricken hearts, beating abnormally from the many long years of physical subjugation. I constantly question myself as to what can I do to ease their pain and elevate their minds? But the crushing reality is this: I cannot help those who refuse to help themselves! Despair has caused these men to give up all their will to fight and struggle on. But I will never be counted among the broken men.

To the incarcerated reading this book, we have no excuses to dwell in idleness. Yes, there could/should be many more positive programs available to us behind these prison walls. We should have access to trade schools, college courses, etc. But what are we doing to achieve these victories? First, we need to utilize the crumbs which we already have on our plates (the limited programs available to us). Next, we must reach out to those in a position to help us and bring awareness to our needs. We all want to get out of prison. But get out and do what? What are we doing right now to make our lives worth living for?

A FEW QUOTES TO MEDITATE ON:
ALL BY, VIKTOR FRANKL

"Everything can be taken from a man but one thing; the last of the human freedoms — to choose one's attitude in any given set of circumstances, to choose one's own way."

"When we are no longer able to change a situation, we are challenged to change ourselves."

"Between stimulus and response there is a space. In that space is our power to choose our response. In our response lies our growth and our freedom."

"Each man is questioned by life; and he can only answer to life by answering for his own life; to life he can only respond by being responsible."

"What is to give light must endure burning."

"Live as if you were living a second time, and as though you had acted wrongly the first time."
"Those who have a 'why' to live can bear with almost any 'how'."

"I grasped the meaning of the greatest secret that human poetry and human thought and belief have to impart: The salvation of man is through love and in love."

"Ever more people today have the means to live, but no meaning to live for."
(Viktor Frankl)

My journey continues... (Davon McNeil)

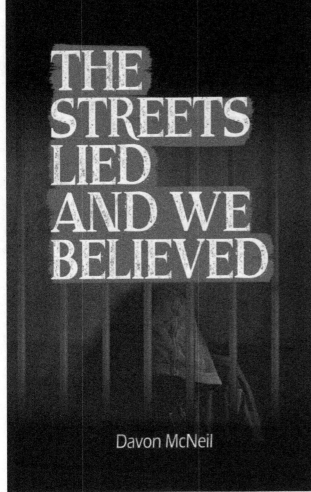

Made in the USA
Coppell, TX
25 August 2022